Express Ahead

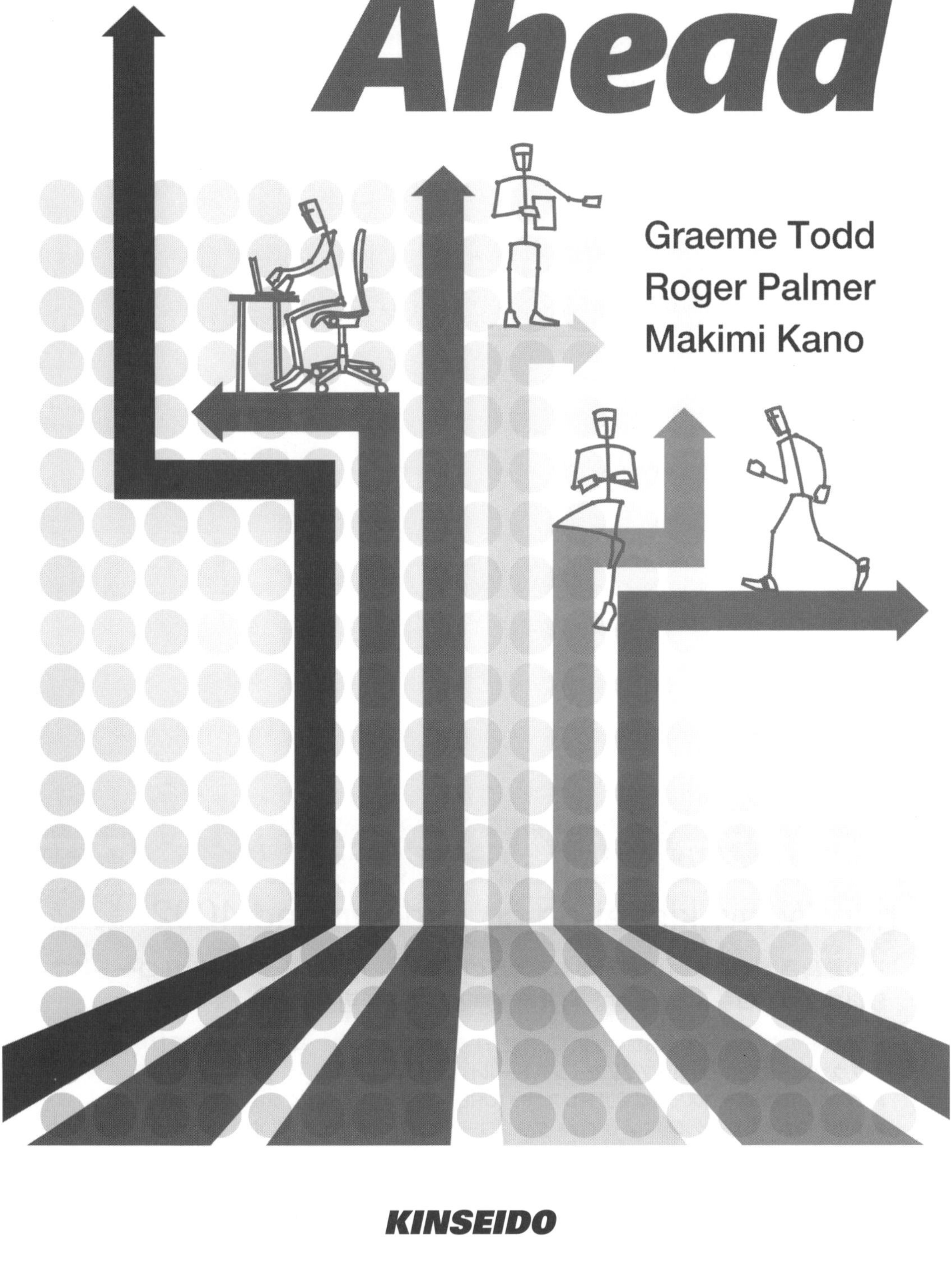

Graeme Todd
Roger Palmer
Makimi Kano

KINSEIDO

Kinseido Publishing Co., Ltd.
3-21 Kanda Jimbo-cho, Chiyoda-ku,
Tokyo 101-0051, Japan

Copyright © 2015 by Graeme Todd
　　　　　　　　Roger Palmer
　　　　　　　　Makimi Kano

All rights reserved. No part of this publication may be reproduced, stored in a retrieval system, or transmitted, in any form or by any means, electronic, mechanical, photocopying, recording or otherwise, without the prior permission of the publisher.

First published 2015 by Kinseido Publishing Co., Ltd.

Acknowledgment
Cover design　　　sein
Text design　　　 sein
Illustrations　　　Atsuko Minato

音声ファイル無料ダウンロード

http://www.kinsei-do.co.jp/download/4002

この教科書で 🎧 DL 00 の表示がある箇所の音声は、上記 URL または QR コードにて無料でダウンロードできます。自習用音声としてご活用ください。

▶ PCからのダウンロードをお勧めします。スマートフォンなどでダウンロードされる場合は、ダウンロード前に「解凍アプリ」をインストールしてください。
▶ URL は、検索ボックスではなくアドレスバー（URL 表示欄）に入力してください。
▶ お使いのネットワーク環境によっては、ダウンロードできない場合があります。

🅒 CD 00　左記の表示がある箇所の音声は、教室用 CD（Class Audio CD）に収録されています。

はじめに

Express Ahead へようこそ！　本書は大学一般教養レベルの英語ライティング・クラスを念頭に置いて執筆しました．このテキストの目標は，学習者のライティング・スキル向上の旅がスムーズで実りあるものになるよう，ガイドの役割を果たすことです．私たち著者の指導経験から，次のような特色が語学学習の成功の一助となると考え，本書に盛り込みました．

本書では，各ユニットの冒頭に，大学生の興味を引くような様々なテーマを取り上げた文章（**Text**）を提示します．文章は大学生の語学レベルに合わせて語彙や表現が調整されています．トピックはライフスタイル，健康，環境，時事問題など多岐に渡り，重要な語彙には語注が付けられています（**Glossary**）．

本書の 24 ユニットはどれもトピックと言語表現がしっかりと結びつけられていて，エクササイズはすべて各章のテーマ，語彙，文法に関するものです．内容理解の質問（**Understanding**）で本文の理解を確認し，コロケーションのエクササイズ（**Collocation Finder**）では語と語の繋がりに焦点をあてた学習を行い，そのユニットで取り上げる文法項目の説明（**Grammar Watch**）に続いて，エクササイズ（**Grammar Try Out**）で文法項目がしっかり理解できたかを確認します．

各ユニットはインプット（読み）からアウトプット（書き）へと自然に移行しています．インプットは，冒頭の文章（**Text**）に加えて，日本語での文法項目の説明（**Grammar Watch**）によって行われます．一方，アウトプットは，答えがある程度決まっているエクササイズ（**Grammar Try Out**, **Checkpoint**）から，オープンエンドなもの（**Guided Practice**, **Open Practice**）へと繋がっていきます．学習者は英語を活用して，自分の考えを言い表すことができるようになるよう自然な流れに乗って，無理なく学習を進められます．

本書は学習者が使用しやすいように構成されています．教材を十分に理解し，課題に取り組めるよう，随所に日本語サポートを組み込んでいます．さらには，エクササイズに取り組むときにページをめくって情報を探したりする必要がないように，ページのレイアウトにも配慮がされています．

最後になりましたが，私たち著者は，*Express Ahead* を使って指導をされる先生方と学習をされる学生さん達の両方が本書を楽しみ，各自の目標達成へと近づかれることを願ってやみません．

著者一同

Contents

Unit	Title	Grammar	Page
1	First Impressions	冠詞	2
2	Sparks at Fuji Rock	可算名詞・不可算名詞	6
3	A Stroke of Luck	名詞の変則的な単数形・複数形	10
4	Keeping Fit, Eating Well	コロケーション（連語）	14
5	Advice to Freshmen	比較級と最上級	18
6	A Cry for Help	感情を表す形容詞	22
7	Festivals	頻度を表す副詞	26
8	A Tasty and Easy Meal	語の選択	30
9	The Tour de France	動詞の過去形	34
10	Clean Water	現在完了	38
11	Women in Work	過去形と現在完了形	42
12	Controversy	句動詞	46

Unit	Title	Grammar	Page
13	The Millennial Generation	未来を表すbe going toとwill	50
14	The Key to Long Life	能力・可能性のcanとcould	54
15	The Future of Tourism	推量のmayとmight	58
16	Cheaper Travel	義務・必要を表す shouldとmust	62
17	Word of the Year	Wh-疑問文	66
18	Considering Others	丁寧な疑問文	70
19	Healthy Grades	時と場所を表す前置詞	74
20	A History of the Internet	前置詞 by, during, for	78
21	The Statistics of Safety	手段・方法のby	82
22	Learn from the Masters	条件のif	86
23	New Technology	伝達のthat	90
24	Rating Professors	理由のbecause	94

UNIT 1

First Impressions

冠詞

Overview

人の第一印象は主に見た目で決まると言われています．この Unit では，印象をよくするための服装についてのアドバイスを読みます．a/an と the の使い方に注意して，次の文章を読みましょう．

Text DL 02　CD 02

　　Mark Twain, **the** American author and greatest humorist of his age, famously said, "Clothes make **the** man. Naked people have little or no influence in society."

　　Of course Twain was joking, but only to make **the** important point that
5　we tend to judge people by appearances. In fact some experts claim that 55% of **the** first impression we make is based on how we look, 38% on how we act, and only 7% on what we say.

　　Assuming you want to make **a** good first impression, **the** first step is to dress appropriately. Wear **a** suit for **a** formal occasion, jeans for **a** casual
10　event, and make sure your clothes fit perfectly. No one looks their best in clothes that are too big or too tight.

　　Also remember to think head to toe. You are one package and people will notice your hair as well as your shoes. Make sure both are at least clean and tidy and, if possible, up to date.

15　　So, dress to impress because, as **the** saying goes, you never get **a** second chance to make **a** great first impression.

Glossary
a humorist「ユーモア作家，ひょうきん者」　influence「影響」　an impression「印象」
assuming ...「…とすれば（仮定して）」　formal「正式な，フォーマルな」
a package「ひとまとめのもの，パック」

2

UNIT 1 *First Impressions*

Understanding

英文の内容に関する答えとして正しいものを a〜c の中から選びましょう.

1. What is the main topic of the text?
    a. clothes and first impressions
    b. influencing society
    c. always dressing appropriately
2. What accounts for 45% of a first impression?
    a. a good joke   b. appropriate dress   c. behavior and speech
3. Which word has a similar meaning to 'occasion'?
    a. casual   b. event   c. fit
4. What should be clean and tidy?
    a. jeans and a suit b. hair and shoes   c. your toes
5. What do you never get a second chance to make?
    a. a great suit   b. a pair of shoes   c. a first impression

Collocation Finder DL 03 CD 03

下の囲みの中の語を使って, 英文中で使われているコロケーションを完成させましょう.

> formal   judge   perfectly   important   tidy   make

1. clean and _____

2. to _____ an impression

3. a _____ occasion

4. to fit _____

5. an _____ point

6. to _____ by appearances

3

Grammar Watch 冠詞

a/an, the は名詞の前につける冠詞ですが，日本語には同じようなものがないので，いつ，どれを使ったらいいか難しいですね．ここでは最低限のルールを押さえておきましょう．

- 数えられる名詞には a, an, the, 複数形の -s のいずれかをつける．
- 単数名詞のうち，初めて話題にするもの、特定されていない名詞には a, an をつける．
- 語頭の発音が母音（i, e, a, o, u など）で始まるものには an を，それ以外は a を使う．
- 既に話題に出たもの，あるいは特定されている名詞には the をつける．

「特定されている名詞」という定義は少しわかりにくいですが，例えば，最上級や first, second のような修飾語が付いていて名詞が限定される場合や，あるいは関係代名詞や前置詞句などで後ろから名詞が修飾されている場合があります．

例▶ My sister bought **a** new book. **The** book is interesting.
Mt. Fuji is **the** high**est** mountain in Japan.
The pen **on the desk** is mine.

英語には数えられる名詞と数えられない名詞があり，数えられない名詞には a, an はつきませんが，the は使います．

冠詞は英語を読むときには気にせず読み飛ばしてしまう小さな単語ですが，そこに使われる名詞を限定したり不特定にしたり，細かな意味を持っていますので，これからは，a, an, the に注意して読んでみましょう．英語を書くときに役立ちますよ．

Grammar Try Out

日本語の意味に合うように以下の語句を並べ替え，英文を完成させましょう．

1. マーク・トウェインはこれまでで最も偉大なユーモア作家の一人である．
(greatest humorists ever / Mark Twain / of the / was one)

2. 第一印象をよくするには，その場にふさわしい服を着ることです．
(good / to make / dress appropriately / first impression / a)

3. 結婚式のような場ではスーツを着ましょう．
(wear a suit / occasion / you should / for an / like a wedding)

4. 昨日買ったスーツは私にぴったりだ．
(suit / me perfectly / I bought / the / yesterday / fits)

5. 第一印象をよくするチャンスは 1 回しかありません．
(great first impression / get one / a / chance / to make / you only)

UNIT 1 | First Impressions

Checkpoint

[　　] 内のキーフレーズを使って日本語に合う英文を作りましょう.

1. マーク・トウェインはユーモアを使って重要な点を突いた.　　[make an important point]

   _____

2. カジュアルな集まりなら，ジーンズがちょうどいい.　　[a casual event]

   _____

3. 頭の先からつま先まで格好がつくよう気を抜かないこと.　　[from head to toe]

   _____

4. 服のサイズがぴったりあってこそ見た目が一番よくなる.　　[fit perfectly]

   _____

5. 靴も髪型も，清潔できちんと整えることを忘れずに.　　[clean and tidy]

   _____

Guided Practice

自分で言葉を補って英文を完成させましょう.

1. I think first impressions are _____.

2. I would wear a suit to go to a _____.

3. I wear jeans when I _____.

4. I think judging people by appearances is _____.

5. To make a good first impression on me, you should _____.

Open Practice

この Unit で学んだ文法（冠詞 a/an, the）を使って，質問に答えましょう.

1. What would you wear to go on a date?

   _____

2. What would you wear for an interview?

   _____

3. On what occasion did you want to make a good first impression?

   _____

Sparks at Fuji Rock

可算名詞・不可算名詞

Overview

音楽は人生の楽しみの一つです．この Unit では，ポップバンド Sparks（スパークス）がフジロック・フェスティバルで演奏した時のレビューを読みます．名詞が数えられる名詞として使われているか，数えられない名詞として使われているかに注意して，次の文章を読んでみましょう．

Text DL 04 CD 04

　　Sparks exploded onto the British pop scene in 1974, with an appearance on TV's Top of the Pops. The next day, everyone at home, at **work**, and at school was talking about them. Though originally from America, Sparks went on to become an enormous **success** in the UK and Europe.

5　　Sparks' performance at Fuji Rock tonight showed why they are so important in pop music history. And, speaking personally, it showed me why pop music has been one of my passions since boyhood. Sparks were the act at Fuji Rock which made me cry.

　　A superb band, Sparks were as powerful as ever. Russell, the lead
10 singer, still has the greatest falsetto in rock. Ron still hammers away on his piano. And the music is **art**. The song *Never Turn Your Back on Mother Earth*, released more than thirty years ago, has never sounded better.

　　Seeing Sparks on stage tonight, my eyes flooded with tears as I was overwhelmed by a wave of nostalgia and **joy**. Then the moment passed, like
15 everything does: **success**, failure, happy **times**, sad days, love. Or a Sparks song.

Glossary

to explode「爆発的に人気が出る」　an act「バンド，演者グループ」　superb「超一流の」
to hammer away「がんがん弾く」　released「リリース（発売）された」　overwhelmed「圧倒される」

UNIT 2　*Sparks at Fuji Rock*

Understanding

英文の内容に関する答えとして正しいものを a～c の中から選びましょう.

1. Which word best describes the review?
   a. negative　　　　b. neutral　　　　c. positive
2. How did Sparks first become famous?
   a. by exploding　　b. by working hard　　c. by appearing on TV
3. At what time of day did Sparks perform at Fuji Rock?
   a. in the morning　b. in the evening　　c. in the afternoon
4. How many members of Sparks does the writer mention by name?
   a. two　　　　　　b. three　　　　　c. four
5. In what tone of voice does Russell sing?
   a. low　　　　　　b. angry　　　　　c. high

Collocation Finder

下の囲みの中の語を使って，英文中で使われているコロケーションを完成させましょう.

> talk　　flood　　enormous　　wave　　on　　appearance

1. an _____ success

2. to _____ about

3. a _____ of nostalgia

4. _____ stage

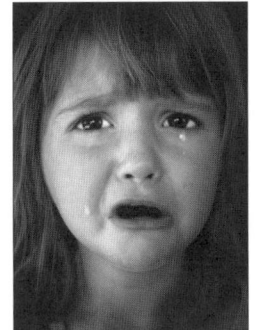
5. a _____ of tears

6. an _____ on TV

7

Grammar Watch　可算名詞・不可算名詞

名詞には，a をつけたり複数形にしたりする可算名詞と，そうはしない不可算名詞があります．抽象概念を表す語や液体，気体，製品の原料，食料品などの物質名詞の多くは不可算名詞です．日本語の感覚では数えられそうな名詞でも，英語では不可算の場合（＝ a をつけたり，複数形にしたりしないもの）があります．これらの数を表すには，piece などを使います．

例▶ information（情報），advice（助言），a piece of furniture（家具），a bar of chocolate，a sheet of paper，a cup of coffee など

一方で，可算名詞としても，不可算名詞としても使われ，それぞれ意味が異なる名詞もあります．例えば，本文の一つ目のパラグラフに出てくる (an enormous) success は「成功者」を表し，可算名詞（an が付いている）ですが，最後のパラグラフに出てくる success は「成功」を意味し，不可算名詞です．ある行為・感情・現象自体は不可算名詞で，その結果産まれる，またはそれらの現象を引き起こす具体物は可算名詞であることが多いのです．辞書では可算名詞は C，不可算名詞は U というラベルで示されます．

例▶ work（U：仕事，C：作品），art（U：芸術，C：芸術作品），joy（U：喜び，C：人を喜ばせるもの），time（U：時刻，C：ひととき，回）など

可算・不可算の区別は日本人学習者にとって難しい概念ですから，簡単な単語でも辞書でそれぞれの使われ方・意味の違いを確認することが重要です．

Grammar Try Out

日本語の意味に合うように以下の語句を並べ替え，英文を完成させましょう．

1. アメリカから来たこのバンドはヨーロッパで成功した．
   (in Europe / band was / a success / this American)

   _____

2. 超一流のアーティスト達が素晴らしい作品を生み出す．
   (produce / superb artists / of art / great works)

   _____

3. 私はポップ・ミュージックに強い思い入れを持っている．
   (a / pop music / passion for / I have)

   _____

4. 週末はリラックスのための時間だ．
   (time / the weekend / for relaxing / is a)

   _____

5. 音楽は私の人生に喜びをもたらしてくれるものの一つだ．
   (of my life / one of the / music is / joys)

   _____

UNIT 2 *Sparks at Fuji Rock*

Checkpoint

[　] 内のキーフレーズを使って日本語に合う英文を作りましょう.

1. スパークスは 1974 年に初めてテレビに出た.　　[on TV]

　_____

2. スパークスがテレビに出てから，誰もが彼らのことを話していた.
　　　　　　　　　　　　　　　　　　　　　[was talking about]

　_____

3. 筆者はスパークスを見て懐かしく思った.　　[a wave of nostalgia]

　_____

4. 彼らの昔の歌は今でもいい曲だ.　　[sound good]

　_____

5. 彼らの日本でのコンサートは大成功だった.　　[an enormous success]

　_____

Guided Practice

自分で言葉を補って英文を完成させましょう.

1. The best live act I have ever seen was _____.

2. I have a passion for _____.

3. For me, music is _____.

4. I feel nostalgic when I think about _____.

5. One of the greatest works of art is _____.

Open Practice

この Unit で学んだ文法（可算名詞・不可算名詞）を使って，質問に答えましょう.

1. What creative art can you do well?

　_____

2. What kind of work do you enjoy?

　_____

3. What thing or activity do you love?

　_____

9

UNIT 3 — A Stroke of Luck

名詞の変則的な単数形・複数形

Overview

誰しも幸運が必要なときがあります．この Unit では電車にカバンを忘れてしまった少年に起きた出来事を取り上げます．名詞の単数形，複数形の使われ方に注意して，次の文章を読んでみましょう．

Text DL 06 CD 06

A couple of weeks ago I left my bag on the train.

I was making my way home after football practice and had all my gear in it, including a new and very expensive **pair of football boots**, some money and my **glasses**. I was exhausted and when the train stopped at my station I got off without thinking.

5　I feared I would never see my stuff again but spoke to **a member of staff** at the station. She was very helpful and reassured me that a lot of lost property is returned every day. Then I went home. My **family** was shocked when I told them the news.

Soon after I got up the next morning I received a phone call. A student had found my bag and handed it in. What a stroke of luck! I fetched my bag and was hugely
10　relieved to discover that nothing was missing. I then called the student. I wanted to buy her a gift to say thank you, but she wouldn't accept anything.

The media frequently criticize young people, saying they don't know how to behave and aren't as principled as people used to be. Well, I think that is nonsense!

Glossary

gear「持ち物，（スポーツ，釣りなど特定の目的に必要な）用具，服装」
exhausted「へとへとに疲れて（exhaust の過去分詞）」　to fear「恐れる」　to reassure「安心させる」
relieved「安心した（relieve の過去分詞）」　principled「道徳心のある，正直な」

UNIT 3 | *A Stroke of Luck*

Understanding

英文の内容に関する答えとして正しいものを a〜c の中から選びましょう.

1. Where was the writer going when he lost his things?
   a. to football practice   b. to the station   c. home
2. Who did the writer speak to at the station?
   a. a member of staff   b. his family   c. a policeman
3. What was not in the bag?
   a. some money   b. a mobile phone   c. a pair of glasses
4. Who found the bag?
   a. the media   b. a student   c. a member of staff
5. What does the writer think of young people?
   a. They behave badly.   b. They make no sense.   c. They are principled.

Collocation Finder   DL 07   CD 07

下の囲みの中の語を使って, 英文中で使われているコロケーションを完成させましょう.

| hugely   accept   receive   frequently   get off   lost |

1. _____ a train

2. _____ criticize

3. _____ relieved

4. _____ property

5. _____ a phone call

6. _____ a gift

11

Grammar Watch　名詞の変則的な単数形・複数形

　可算名詞には，単数形と複数形があり，通例一つのものを指すときには単数形，二つかそれ以上のものを指すときには複数形が用いられます．複数形は語尾に -s をつけて作る場合と不規則変化の場合があります．中には形は複数形なのに一つのものを指すこともものがあります．これは，一見一つのものでも，左右に一つずつの部分があって繋がっている場合に多く見られます．この種の名詞は pair を使って数を表します．

例▶ a pair of glasses （めがね），a pair of scissors （はさみ），two pairs of trousers （ズボン）

　日本語ではシューズ，ブーツ，ソックスと複数形の形でしか使われないこれらの単語も，元は shoe, boot, sock を複数形で使って一足を表したものです．上記の場合と同じように pair を使って数を表します．一つのものを指す場合，pair of を使うかどうかで，動詞が変わります．

例▶ These glasses **are** for reading. / This pair of glasses **is** for reading.
　　　（これは読書用のめがねです．）

　逆のケースとしては，単数形の名詞が，実は複数のものを指していることがあります．複数の人を1グループとしてまとめて捉えているのです．

例▶ family （家族），staff （スタッフ，職員），people （人々），police （警察）

　family や staff は見た目は単数形ですが，それらが主語で用いられ，一人ひとりを指す場合動詞は複数形（be 動詞なら are, were, 一般動詞なら 3 単現の -s はつけない）を使うこともあります．

Grammar Try Out

日本語の意味に合うように以下の語句を並べ替え，英文を完成させましょう．

1. カバンにはサッカー用の靴が一足入っていました．
   (was / a pair / in the bag / of football boots)

2. いつもメガネをかけているわけではありません．
   (wear / I don't / all the time / glasses)

3. スタッフの一人に元気づけられました．
   (by a / I was / of staff / member / reassured)

4. 家族はその知らせを聞いてショックを受けました．
   (shocked when they / heard the news / was / my family)

5. マスコミでは，若者は行儀作法を知らないと言われています．
   (don't know / young people / the media say / how to behave)

UNIT 3 | *A Stroke of Luck*

Checkpoint

[　] 内のキーフレーズを使って日本語に合う英文を作りましょう

1. 夜遅く，電話がかかってきました．　　[a phone call]

_____

2. 私は持ち物全部をカバンに入れました．　　[all my gear]

_____

3. なくしたものが戻って来てラッキーでした．　　[lost property]

_____

4. 私は家族によく非難されます．　　[my family]

_____

5. あの親切な女性に会えたのは運がよかった．　　[a stroke of luck]

_____

Guided Practice

自分で言葉を補って英文を完成させましょう．

1. I once lost _____.

2. In my bag I always keep _____.

3. I get exhausted when I _____.

4. I don't like it when people _____.

5. I think young people today are _____.

Open Practice

この Unit で学習した文法（名詞の単数形・複数形）を使って，質問に答えましょう．

1. What things would you hate to lose?

_____

2. What do you think of the behavior of young people?

_____

3. Did you ever have a stroke of luck? What happened?

_____

13

UNIT 4 Keeping Fit, Eating Well

コロケーション（連語）

Overview

冬の間は体調管理，健康維持が難しいという人は多くいます．この Unit は運動・食事についてのアドバイスです．「コロケーション」（連語）に注目して記事を読んでみましょう．

Text DL 08　CD 08

　　In winter, the chance of **catching a cold** increases and it is all the more important to **keep fit** and healthy.

　　People who want to **feel good** and **stay in shape** during this season need to **take regular exercise**. Everyone can enjoy taking a walk, **going**
5 **for a bicycle ride** or jogging in their local park. And in cities where it can be more difficult to find a safe place for recreation, health clubs and gyms have become popular places to exercise or just hang out.

　　But in addition to exercise you also need to watch what you eat. Especially in winter, when it is cold and people tend to stay home, it is easy
10 to **put on weight** by eating more than you really need. Children often eat snacks between meals, but for adults this is **a bad habit**. The body does not need those extra calories and snacks can be bad for the digestion.

　　Eventually spring comes around and it becomes easier to **lose weight**. The days are longer, the weather is warmer and people tend to be more
15 active. This is the perfect time for even couch potatoes to shed a few pounds!

Glossary

recreation「レクリエーション，気晴らし」　to hang out「ぶらぶらする」　a calorie「カロリー」　digestion「消化」　a couch potato「カウチポテト（＝ごろごろしてテレビばかり見ている人）」　to shed a few pounds「体重を少し落とす」

14

UNIT 4 *Keeping Fit, Eating Well*

Understanding

英文の内容に関する答えとして正しいものをa〜cの中から選びましょう.

1. When are colds more likely?
   a. in winter　　　　b. in cities　　　　c. in spring
2. What helps people feel good?
   a. hanging out　　　b. regular exercise　c. snacks
3. Where can people safely take regular exercise?
   a. in the city　　　b. in a local park　c. at health clubs and gyms
4. Who should not eat snacks between meals?
   a. children　　　　b. adults　　　　　c. doctors
5. Why is it easier to lose weight in spring?
   a. People stop eating.　b. Food tastes better.　c. People are more active.

Collocation Finder  DL 09　 CD 09

下の囲みの中の語を使って，英文中で使われているコロケーションを完成させましょう.

> take　　put on　　catch　　stay　　go　　feel

1. to _____ for a ride　2. to _____ exercise　3. to _____ good

4. to _____ weight　5. to _____ a cold　6. to _____ in shape

15

Grammar Watch　コロケーション（連語）

　ある二つまたはそれ以上の一群の語が，繰り返し同じ並びで使われることをコロケーションといいます．単語を一つずつ覚えるより，その語と共に使われる語をセットでコロケーションとして覚えることで，語彙力がアップするだけでなく，より自然な英語を身につけることができます．
　語と語の結びつきの種類は様々ありますが，主に名詞を中心に考えるとわかりやすいでしょう．ある名詞がどのような動詞・形容詞・前置詞と一緒に使われるのか知っていると便利です．例えば，本文に出てくる「運動」という意味の exercise は get や take という動詞を伴って，「運動をする」という意味になります．日本語ではスポーツの種類はおおよそどれでも「する」という動詞を使いますが，英語ではすべてが do というわけではありません．

例▶
- 球技には play を使う（play tennis/golf/football など）．
- 武道には do や practice を使う（do judo/karate など）．
- スキーやスケートのように日本語ではスポーツ名として使われる語そのものが動詞として使われる（ski, skate, swim, run など）．

　日本語の「する」に引きずられて do ski などと言ったり，play tennis などの表現をまねて play judo などと言うと不自然な英語になってしまうのです．
　知らない単語が出てきて辞書を引くときには，その語の意味だけではなく，一緒に使われる語も確認し，コロケーションとして覚えていきましょう．

Grammar Try Out

コロケーションを意識しながら日本語の意味に合うように以下の語句を並べ替え，英文を完成させましょう．

1. 冬はとても風邪を引きやすい季節です．
   (it is / a cold in winter / to catch / very easy)

   _____

2. 冬の間，体調を維持するのは大切だ．
   (important / to keep / it is / fit during winter)

   _____

3. 定期的な運動をすると，人は気分がよくなります．
   (regular / feel good / people to / exercise helps)

   _____

4. 間食はよくない習慣です．
   (habit / eating snacks / is a bad / between meals)

   _____

5. カウチポテト族にとっては，春は減量しやすい季節です．
   (weight in spring / find it / easier to lose / couch potatoes)

   _____

UNIT 4 | Keeping Fit, Eating Well

Checkpoint

[　] 内のキーフレーズを使って日本語に合う英文を作りましょう.

1. 体形を保つため定期的に運動をしています.　　[**regular exercise**]

_____

2. 週に2回, サイクリングをします.　　[**go for a ride**]

_____

3. ジョギングをすると気分がいいです.　　[**feel good**]

_____

4. カウチポテト族はテレビの前に座って, たくさん食べます.　　[**couch potatoes**]

_____

5. 春には体重を少し落とさなきゃ.　　[**shed a few pounds**]

_____

Guided Practice

自分で言葉を補って英文を完成させましょう.

1. A good way to keep fit in winter is to _____.

2. In summer I like to take exercise _____.

3. I feel good when I _____.

4. I think people put on weight because _____.

5. The easiest way to lose weight is to _____.

Open Practice

この Unit に出てきたコロケーションを使って, 質問に応えましょう.

1. What makes you feel good?

_____

2. Do you have any bad eating habits? What are they?

_____

3. What do you do to avoid catching colds?

_____

17

Advice to Freshmen

比較級と最上級

Overview

新入生は大学に入学することにわくわくすると同時に不安を感じることも多いでしょう．このUnitには入学後の最初の数週間を乗り切るためのアドバイスが書かれています．比較級・最上級に特に注意しながら，次の文章を読みましょう．

Text DL 10 CD 10

What could be **more exciting** than entering university? But what could be **more nerve-racking**? Keep the following pieces of advice in mind and your first few weeks in college could be the **greatest** experience of your life.

Make friends slowly. The people you meet on your first day don't have to become your **best** friends. Be friendly, but keep an open mind.

Budget properly. All but the **wealthiest** students must be careful with their money so don't waste it. Have a clear idea of what you need to spend on food, socializing, and materials for study. You will be much **happier** if you have money left at the end of the semester.

Don't feel ashamed about missing home. For students living away from home, homesickness is natural. Discuss it with your new friends. They will almost certainly have the same feelings.

Get involved. Get involved in college life at the **earliest** opportunity. Take an interest in student societies and clubs. Listen to what they have to say and go along to some meetings.

Enjoy yourself. You will only be at college for a few short years so make sure you enjoy it!

Glossary

nerve-racking「神経を使う，気疲れする」　an open mind「広い心」
to budget「予算を立てる，お金の計画をする（動詞），予算，生活費（名詞）」
socializing「交友，友達との付き合い」　ashamed「恥ずかしい」
to go along to「～へ行く，～に参加する」

18

UNIT 5　Advice to Freshmen

Understanding

英文の内容に関する答えとして正しいものを a〜c の中から選びましょう.

1. Which words are used to describe entering university?
   a. more or less
   b. slowly and properly
   c. exciting and nerve-racking
2. How many pieces of advice are given in the article?
   a. five　　　　　　b. six　　　　　　c. seven
3. How should students deal with homesickness?
   a. forget it　　　　b. discuss it　　　c. feel ashamed
4. How can students get involved in college life?
   a. by making friends
   b. through clubs and societies
   c. by not wasting money
5. According to the article, for how long do students attend university?
   a. a semester or two　　b. four years　　c. a few short years

Collocation Finder　DL 11　CD 11

下の囲みの中の語を使って, 英文中で使われているコロケーションを完成させましょう.

| home | mind | enter | piece | waste | interest |

1. to _____ university

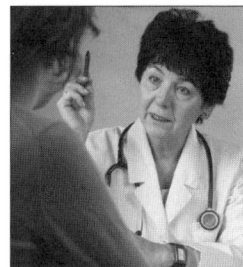

2. a _____ of advice

3. keep it in _____

4. to _____ money

5. away from _____

6. to take an _____

19

Grammar Watch　　比較級と最上級

「○○より△△の方が…」とか「○○の中で△△が一番…」のように二つかそれ以上のものを比較して述べるときに使うのが形容詞・副詞の比較級・最上級です．比較級・最上級は短い語の語尾に -er/-est を付けたり，長い語の前に more/most をつけて作ります．

例▶ great → great**er**/great**est**, small → small**er**/small**est**, easy → eas**ier**/eas**iest**, big → big**ger**/big**gest**, difficult → **more**/**most** difficult

例を見るとわかるように，-er/-est をつけるときに語尾の -y を -i に変えたり，語尾の子音字を重ねたりするものもありますし，-er/-est をつけるか more/most をつけるかわからない場合もあるでしょう．また，原級と全く異なる比較級の形を持つ形容詞・副詞もあります．その都度辞書で正しい形を確認しましょう．

例▶ good → better/best, bad → worse/worst, little → less/least

二つのものを比較して「○○より△△の方が…」と言うには［比較級 + than］を用います．

例▶ • To me, biology is **more interesting than** chemistry.（私には化学より生物学の方がおもしろい．）

二つ以上のものを比べて「○○の中で△△が一番…」と言うときには［the + 最上級］を用います．

例▶ • Mt. Fuji is **the highest** mountain in Japan.（富士山は日本で一番高い山だ．）

Grammar Try Out

日本語の意味に合うように以下の語句を並べ替え，英文を完成させましょう．

1. 大学は高校より楽しいと思う．
(is more / university / I think / high school / exciting than)

2. 大学生活が人生で一番の経験だったとよく言われる．
(that university was / people often say / experience of their life / the greatest)

3. 最も裕福な層の学生はお金のことを気にしなくてよい．
(about money / students don't / the wealthiest / have to worry)

4. 多少のお金があったほうが，たいていの人はうれしい．
(people happier / having / makes most / some money)

5. できるだけ早い時期にクラブに入ることを勧められた．
(a club / I was advised / opportunity / at the earliest / to join)

UNIT 5 | Advice to Freshmen

Checkpoint

[　] 内のキーフレーズを使って日本語に合う英文を作りましょう．

1. 大学のおかげで新しい考え方に心を開くことができた． [opened my mind]

   _____

2. 一番のお金持ちが一番の幸せ者とは限らない． [the happiest people]

   _____

3. 大学生活最初の週はたくさんの集まりに参加した． [went along to]

   _____

4. 英語より中国語の方が難しい言語だと思う． [more difficult]

   _____

5. 本を買うことは決してお金の無駄にはならない． [a waste of money]

   _____

Guided Practice

自分で言葉を補って英文を完成させましょう．

1. Sometimes I waste money on _____.

2. The greatest experience of my life was _____.

3. My mind was opened by _____.

4. I take an interest in _____.

5. The most difficult thing I have ever done was _____.

Open Practice

この Unit で学んだ文法（比較級・最上級）を使って，質問に答えましょう．

1. What makes you feel both excited and nervous at the same time?

   _____

2. Do you think it is more important to get an interesting job or a high salary?

   _____

3. What advice would you give a student on their first day at your school?

   _____

UNIT 6 — A Cry for Help

感情を表す形容詞

Overview

この Unit では，一人の少年が母親との関係に悩んでアドバイスを求めています．-ed，-ing で終わる形容詞に注意しながら，次の文章を読んでみましょう．

Text   DL 12   CD 12

Dear Meg,

My nosy mom is wearing me out! What are you doing? Where are you going? Have you finished your homework? I'm **tired** of hearing such questions. She still treats me like a kid and has no respect for my privacy. To tell the truth, it's **tiring** being in the
5 same house as her.

She can be an **embarrassing** gossip too. One day I told her something about one of my friends at school. I couldn't believe it when she went and told my friend's mom exactly what I had said. I don't think she understands how **embarrassed** I felt about that. And what's more, my friend is now ignoring me.

10 I try to keep calm but this situation is really **annoying** me. It gets me down and I don't think I can stand it for much longer. I get so **annoyed** answering the same questions over and over again. I try to hide my anger but sometimes I can't think about anything else and explode.

She's **frustrating**, I'm **frustrated**, and I really don't know what I can do to improve
15 our relationship. Of course I love my mom dearly, but she's driving me crazy!
I hope you can help.
Yours sincerely,
A frustrated teenager

Glossary

nosy「詮索好きな，おせっかいな」　respect for「（意見など）に対する尊重・敬意」
to ignore「無視する」　to stand「耐える」　to explode「爆発する」　dearly「心から」

UNIT 6 *A Cry for Help*

Understanding

英文の内容に関する答えとして正しいものを a ～ c の中から選びましょう.

1. Who is the writer mainly writing about?
   a. his friend's mom
   b. his mom
   c. his friends
2. What does the writer call his mom?
   a. a friend
   b. a kid
   c. a gossip
3. Who has stopped talking to the writer?
   a. his mom
   b. his friend
   c. Meg
4. Has the writer ever lost his temper?
   a. yes
   b. not yet
   c. no
5. Why has the writer written this letter?
   a. for homework
   b. to calm down
   c. to ask for help

Collocation Finder

下の囲みの中の語を使って，英文中で使われているコロケーションを完成させましょう.

| dearly | calm | relationship | out | privacy | crazy |

1. respect for _____

2. to drive (someone) _____

3. to wear (someone) _____

4. to love (someone) _____

5. to keep _____

6. to improve a _____

23

Grammar Watch　　感情を表す形容詞

わくわくする，イライラするなど，感情を表す形容詞には，元々「～させる」という意味の動詞に -ed や -ing を付け形容詞として使われるというタイプのものが多くあります．人の感情を表すときには -ed，人をそのような感情にさせる事・物・人などを形容するときに -ing を付けます．

例▶

動詞（…させる）	形容詞（人が…）	形容詞（物事が…）
surprise（びっくりさせる）	surprised（驚いた）	surprising（びっくりするような）
excite（わくわくさせる）	excited（わくわくしている）	exciting（わくわくするような）
annoy（イライラさせる）	annoyed（イライラする）	annoying（イライラさせるような）

以下の例文で，主語と -ed, -ing の関係を確認しましょう．

例▶　I am excit*ed* about the party.　⇔　The party is excit*ing*.
　　　（私＝わくわくしている．パーティ＝私をわくわくさせている．）
　　　I am interest*ed* in the new book.　⇔　The new book is interest*ing*.
　　　（私＝興味を持っている．新しい本＝興味深い）

映画などが面白くなくて「つまんない」と言おうとして，"I'm boring." と言ってしまうと，「私は退屈な人間です」と言っていることになってしまいますのでご注意を．

Grammar Try Out

日本語の意味に合うように以下の語句を並べ替え，英文を完成させましょう．

1. 母親と一緒に暮らすのは疲れる．
   (is / tiring / my mom / living with)

   _____

2. 母が私のことを人に話したとき，とっても恥ずかしかった．
   (about me / I felt / she talked / so embarrassed when / to other people)

   _____

3. 母が私のことを人に話すと，ばつが悪い．
   (other people / embarrassing when / about me / it is / she speaks to)

   _____

4. 母の質問は気にしないようにしている．
   (not to / her questions / I try / get annoyed / with)

   _____

5. 母の質問はとってもイライラする．
   (annoying / so / her / questions are)

   _____

UNIT 6 | *A Cry for Help*

Checkpoint

[　] 内のキーフレーズを使って日本語に合う英文を作りましょう．

1. 両親は私に恥ずかしい思いをさせたことがない．　　[embarrassed me]

　_____

2. 私は両親をやっかいだとは思わない．　　[very embarrassing]

　_____

3. 私は疲れると怒りっぽくなる．　　[get annoyed]

　_____

4. 宿題が終わらなくて嫌気がさした．　　[was frustrated]

　_____

5. 宿題にはひどくストレスを感じるときがある．　　[really frustrating]

　_____

Guided Practice

自分で言葉を補って英文を完成させましょう．

1. I am tired of _____.

2. The most tiring day of my week is _____.

3. I get frustrated by _____.

4. One thing I find really annoying is _____.

5. When you feel annoyed, my advice is to _____.

Open Practice

この Unit で学んだ文法（感情を表す形容詞）を使って，質問に答えましょう．

1. What situations do you find really embarrassing?

　_____

2. What do you do to calm down when you get annoyed?

　_____

3. What advice would you give to a friend who feels frustrated?

　_____

UNIT 7 Festivals

頻度を表す副詞

Overview

たいていの人はお祭りに行くのが好きです．この Unit では世界の最も有名でわくわくする祭りの中から 3 つの祭りを紹介します．頻度を表す副詞に注意しながら，次の文章を読んでみましょう．

Text DL 14 CD 14

Do you **occasionally** hanker after an unforgettable experience? Do you like the excitement of a good festival? These festivals are held **annually** and each offers something unique. Why not visit one?

The Edinburgh Festival Fringe is the world's largest arts festival. Over 25,000 artists
5 come together **every August** in Scotland to perform music, dance, children's shows, comedy and more. During the festival the city doesn't sleep. There is **always** something happening.

Over in Italy, the Carnival of Venice is famous for masks and attracts 3 million visitors **every year**. During the carnival, Venice comes alive with bands and entertainers.
10 Colorful boats fill the canals and **every night** there are parties and balls. People **often** say the carnival feels like a fairy tale come to life.

Mardi Gras festivals are held all over Europe, but the liveliest of all is in the American city of New Orleans. Mardi Gras, which means Fat Tuesday, refers to the eating of fatty food before fasting. There is **usually** one major parade a day and people
15 **frequently** dress in outrageous costumes. You **regularly** hear it said that Mardi Gras is for those who can't wait for Halloween to look ridiculous!

Glossary

to hanker after「あこがれる，欲しいと思う」 annually「毎年」
a ball「ダンスパーティ，舞踏会」 a carnival「謝肉祭（四旬節の前に肉を食べ楽しく過ごすキリスト教の行事）」 fasting「断食」 outrageous「突飛な，あきれるほどの」

UNIT 7 *Festivals*

Understanding

英文の内容に関する答えとして正しいものを a ～ c の中から選びましょう

1. How many famous European festivals does the article introduce?
   a. two   b. three   c. four
2. How often are these festivals held?
   a. every year   b. every four years   c. every decade
3. Where is Edinburgh?
   a. in Italy   b. in the USA   c. in Scotland
4. At which festival do people wear shocking clothes?
   a. Edinburgh   b. Venice   c. Mardi Gras
5. At which festival do people cover their faces?
   a. Edinburgh   b. Venice   c. Mardi Gras

Collocation Finder DL 15 CD 15

下の囲みの中の語を使って，英文中で使われているコロケーションを完成させましょう．

| for   food   arts   dress in   held   unforgettable |

1. an _____ experience

2. famous _____ (something)

3. festivals are _____

4. fatty _____

5. to _____ costumes

6. an _____ festival

27

Grammar Watch　　頻度を表す副詞

頻度を表すには副詞や副詞の役割をする句を使います．基本的なものを以下に挙げます．
- always（いつも），usually（たいてい），often（しばしば），sometimes（時々），never（一度もない）

これらの語は，主語の後，一般動詞の前，be 動詞の後に置かれます．

例▶ My brother **often** gets mad at me.（お兄ちゃんはよく私に腹を立てる．）
　　　My room is **always** a mess.（私の部屋はいつも散らかっている．）

それ以外にも頻度を表す副詞（句）はたくさんあります．
- all the time（いつも），almost always（たいてい），frequently, regularly（しょっちゅう），occasionally, once in a while, from time to time（時折），seldom, rarely, hardly ever, almost never（滅多にない）

定期的に繰り返される習慣・行為を表すのもこのグループの副詞です．
- daily, weekly, monthly, yearly, annually, every day/week/month/year（毎日・毎週・毎月・毎年）

これらのうち，下線を引いた語句は上の基本的な5つと同じ位置で使いますが，それ以外は文の後ろの方に来ることが多いです．

例▶ She **rarely** complains.（彼女は滅多に不満を言わない．）
　　　Come visit us **once in a while**.（たまには顔出してね．）

Grammar Try Out

日本語の意味に合うように以下の語句を並べ替え，英文を完成させましょう

1. エディンバラ・フェスティバル・フリンジは毎年スコットランドで開催される．
   (annually in / is held / the Edinburgh Festival Fringe / Scotland)

2. ほとんどの人は，時にはちょっとしたドキドキが欲しいと思うものです．
   (almost / hankers after / a little excitement / everyone occasionally)

3. マルディグラではあっけにとられるようなコスチュームを着ている人をよく見かける．
   (see people / dressed in / Mardi Gras / you frequently / outrageous costumes at)

4. ヴェネツィア・カーニバルでは，人々は仮面をかぶることがよくある．
   (often wear / Carnival of Venice / masks / at the / people)

5. マルディグラでは毎日大きなパレードが行われる．
   (parade every day / a major / there is / Mardi Gras / at)

UNIT 7 *Festivals*

Checkpoint

[　] 内のキーフレーズを使って日本語に合う英文を作りましょう.

1. エディンバラはスコットランドの首都として有名だ.　　[famous for]

　_____

2. 世界最大の芸術の祭典ではいつも何かが行われている.

　　　　　　　　　　　　　　　　　　　　[something happening]

　_____

3. マルディグラの間, ニューオリンズは盛り上がる.　　[comes alive]

　_____

4. 祭りが楽しいと人はたいてい盛り上がるものだ.　　[usually enjoy]

　_____

5. 人々は突飛な衣装を着ていたので, こっけいに見えた.　　[looked ridiculous]

　_____

Guided Practice

自分で言葉を補って英文を完成させましょう.

1. I had an unforgettable experience when I _____.

2. I would like to visit _____.

3. One festival I'm not interested in is _____.

4. The last festival I went to was _____.

5. The last time I wore a mask was _____.

Open Practice

この Unit で学習した文法（頻度を表す副詞）を使って, 質問に答えましょう.

1. How often do you go to a festival?

　_____

2. Do you have a favorite festival? What do you like about it?

　_____

3. How often do you hanker after a new experience?

　_____

A Tasty and Easy Meal

語の選択

Overview

料理は難しいし時間がかかると思っている人もいるでしょう。そこで，この Unit では簡単においしいパスタソースを作る方法を紹介します。調理に関する語彙に注目しながら，次の文章を読んでみましょう．

Text

Pasta sauces make brilliantly tasty and easy meals. And they taste even more delicious if you use fresh ingredients. This is not always possible, but you should definitely try.

One classic pasta sauce is called pesto. Once you have bought the
5 ingredients, this dish only takes about 10 minutes to prepare. Here is the recipe.

First, **pound** two tablespoons of olive oil, one garlic clove (quartered), and four tablespoons of **chopped** basil in a mortar. Then **beat in** three more tablespoons of olive oil. Next, add a teaspoon of salt, four tablespoons
10 of **chopped** parsley, and a quarter of a teaspoon of freshly **grated** nutmeg. **Pound** the mixture in your mortar until it is reduced to a paste. Finally, **stir in** about 30g of **grated** Parmesan cheese.

When the sauce is ready all you need to do is simply **toss** cooked pasta in the pesto and sit down to a tasty and healthy meal!

15 After you have finished eating, there are not even that many dishes to wash. Yet another advantage of making pesto!

Glossary

to pound「すりつぶす」 a mortar「すり鉢」 to beat in「(主に泡立て器で，卵・油など) を入れてかきまぜる」 to reduce to「(煮詰まったり，すりつぶされたりして) 〜の状態になる」
to stir in「〜に入れてかき混ぜる」 to toss「〜を軽く和える」

UNIT 8 *A Tasty and Easy Meal*

Understanding

英文の内容に関する答えとして正しいものを a～c の中から選びましょう.

1. Which word best describes the article?
   a. a recipe   b. a meal   c. a story
2. How is pesto described?
   a. chopped   b. fresh   c. classic
3. Which ingredient is not used to make pesto?
   a. cheese   b. meat   c. salt
4. How is the mixture reduced to a paste?
   a. It is pounded.   b. It is chopped.   c. It is tossed.
5. What else is good about making pesto?
   a. It is cheap.   b. few dishes to wash   c. Tossing pasta is simple.

Collocation Finder DL 17 CD 17

下の囲みの中の語を使って，英文中で使われているコロケーションを完成させましょう.

fresh   grated   prepare   add   tasty   sauce

1. to _____ salt

2. _____ cheese

3. to _____ a dish

4. a _____ meal

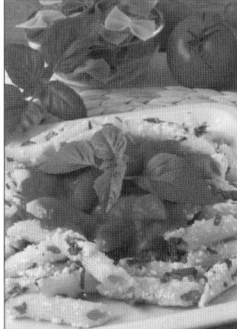
5. pasta _____

6. _____ ingredients

31

Grammar Watch　　語の選択

物事を説明したり，状況を描写したりするときには，できるだけ的確で具体的な語彙を使うことで，情報を正確にわかりやすく伝えることができます．とくに料理のレシピのように，作業に正確性が求められる工程を説明するときには，一つ一つの動作をぴったりと表す語を選んで使わないと，料理が失敗に終わってしまいます．特に，ものを混ぜたりする動作とそのときに使う道具は結びついていることが多いので，セットで覚えるのがよいでしょう．

例▶
- pound: すり鉢（mortar）とすりこぎ（pestle）を使って材料をすりつぶす
- beat in: 泡立て器（beater）を使って，叩くように混ぜる
- stir: スプーンやへら（spatula），菜箸などで混ぜる
- toss: ボウル（bowl）に入った材料を大きなスプーンとフォークなどで軽やかに混ぜる．

また，材料がどのように下ごしらえしてあるかを表現するのには，grated（すり下ろした），chopped（ざく切りにした），mashed（つぶした），minced（みじん切りの）などの動詞の過去分詞が使われます．

料理の成功には，正確な計量も不可欠です．材料の数・量を表す表現も覚えましょう．

例▶　a tablespoon/teaspoon of（大さじ/小さじ一杯），a cup of（1カップ），a clove of（ニンニクなどの一片），a bunch of（葉野菜などの一束，果物などの一房）

Grammar Try Out

日本語の意味に合うように以下の語句を並べ替え，英文を完成させましょう．

1. すり鉢はニンニクなどの材料をすりつぶすのに使われる．
   (such as / is used to / pound ingredients / a mortar / garlic)

2. オリーブオイルや卵などの材料は泡立て器で混ぜ込むとよい．
   (olive oil and eggs / beat in / you can / such as / ingredients)

3. 通常，材料はスプーンで混ぜる．
   (with a spoon / stirred in / ingredients / are usually)

4. チーズやナツメグはすり下ろして使うこともある．
   (can both / nutmeg / be grated / cheese and)

5. パスタはソースとなじませるために，軽く混ぜ合わせることが多い．
   (it in / pasta is / a sauce / to cover / often tossed)

UNIT 8 | *A Tasty and Easy Meal*

Checkpoint

[　] 内のキーフレーズを使って日本語に合う英文を作りましょう.

1. イタリア料理にはおろしたチーズが入っていることが多い.　　[**grated cheese**]

   _____

2. バジルソースはたった 10 分でできます.　　[**prepare pesto**]

   _____

3. このレシピではオリーブオイルを大さじ 5 杯使います.　　[**five tablespoons**]

   _____

4. おいしくてヘルシーな食事を作るのは難しくはありません.　　[**tasty and healthy**]

   _____

5. 食後の洗い物が少ないのはうれしい.　　[**dishes to wash**]

   _____

Guided Practice

自分で言葉を補って英文を完成させましょう.

1. Classic pizza toppings are _____.

2. In salad I like _____.

3. My favorite pasta sauce is _____.

4. Recently I cooked _____.

5. I'd like to try cooking _____.

Open Practice

この Unit で学んだ語彙を使って，質問に答えましょう.

1. What tasty and easy dish can you cook?

   _____

2. How do you make it?

   _____

3. What don't you like about cooking?

   _____

33

UNIT 9 The Tour de France

動詞の過去形

Overview

サイクリングは世界中で人気のスポーツです．この Unit は世界最大の無料スポーツイベントであるツール・ド・フランスについてです．動詞の過去形に注意して，次の文章を読んでみましょう．

Text DL 18 CD 18

One of the most popular spectator sports in the world is cycling, and the world's largest free sporting event is the Tour de France.

The first Tour de France was **held** in 1903. Fewer than 100 cyclists **took part** and it **included** night stages, with some riders breaking the
5 rules in the dark. The winner of this first race **wore** a green armband, but from 1919 the rider who **completed** the race in the fastest time **won** a yellow jersey.

Over the years, the Tour **became** a team race as well as an individual race. It **kept** the yellow jersey and **added** several other jerseys. Green
10 was **introduced** for the points winner, polka dots for the King of the Mountains, and white for the best young rider.

Last year's race **drew** riders from around the world and more than 20 professional teams. They **covered** over 3,000 kilometres in 21 stages and the race **lasted** about three weeks.
15 About 12 million spectators **went** to watch the Tour. Best of all, no one **needed** a ticket.

Glossary
a spectator「観客」 a stage「（ある行程の）段，ステージ」 a jersey「（スポーツ用の）ジャージ」
polka dots「水玉模様」 the King of the Mountains「山岳賞」 to draw「引き寄せる」

UNIT 9 | *The Tour de France*

Understanding

英文の内容に関する答えとして正しいものを a～c の中から選びましょう．

1. What kind of event is the Tour de France?
   a. a car competition   b. a mountain marathon   c. a bicycle race
2. What is true about the Tour de France?
   a. It is free.   b. It is English.   c. It is a night race.
3. Why were night stages a problem?
   a. Some riders cheated.   b. Some riders fell off.   c. Some riders got lost.
4. How many jerseys are mentioned in the article?
   a. three   b. four   c. five
5. Who gets to wear the white jersey?
   a. the points winner
   b. the King of the Mountains
   c. the best young rider

Collocation Finder   DL 19   CD 19

下の囲みの中の語を使って，英文中で使われているコロケーションを完成させましょう．

| fastest   popular   professional   complete   break   sporting |

1. a _____ sport
2. to _____ the rules 
3. the _____ time 
4. to _____ a race 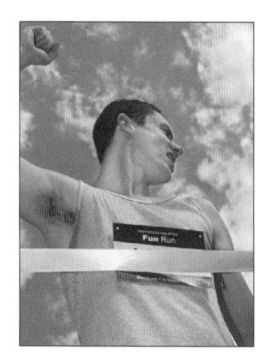
5. a _____ team 
6. a _____ event 

35

Grammar Watch　動詞の過去形

過去の出来事について話すときには動詞を過去形にして使います．一般動詞の過去形の作り方には，一定の規則があります．

- 原則として，動詞の原形に -ed をつける．例：wait → wait**ed**, talk → talk**ed**
- 語尾が -e なら -d のみをつける．例：like → like**d**, taste → taste**d**
- 語尾が -y なら y → ied．例：study → stud**ied**, marry → marr**ied**
  * 語尾の y の前が母音なら -yed．例：enjoy → enjo**yed**, annoy → anno**yed**
- 語尾が短母音+子音なら子音字を重ねて -ed．例：skip → ski**pped**, trek → tre**kked**

一部の一般動詞や be 動詞は不規則に変化します．

- be 動詞：**am/is → was**, **are → were**.
- 一般動詞（不規則変化）：**see → saw**, **shake → shook**, **wear → wore**, **take → took**, **tell → told**

不規則変化する動詞の数は少ないですが，よく使う動詞が多いので基本的なものは辞書の巻末などにある不規則動詞変化表で覚えましょう．規則変化をする動詞でも -ed をつけるという大原則に則る語以外は，辞書を調べれば，正しい形が載っていますので，間違わないようにその都度確認して，覚えていくことが大切です．

Grammar Try Out

日本語の意味に合うように以下の語句を並べ替え，英文を完成させましょう．

1. 史上最大の自転車レースは 1975 年フランスで開催された．
   (France in 1975 / the biggest ever / was held in / bicycle race)

2. すべてのステージで最も早くゴールした選手に賞が与えられた．
   (in the fastest time / all the stages / who completed / won a prize / the rider)

3. 山岳ステージの勝者は水玉模様のジャージを着た．
   (mountain stages / a polka dot jersey / wore / of the / the winner)

4. 約千人の選手が大会に参加した．
   (took part / in the event / a thousand cyclists / around)

5. 約 1200 万人の観客が無料でレースを観戦した．
   (the race for free / about / watched / 12 million spectators)

UNIT 9 | *The Tour de France*

Checkpoint

[　] 内のキーフレーズを使って日本語に合う英文を作りましょう.

1. 第1回ツール・ド・フランスは100年以上前に開催された.　　[was held]

   _____

2. 夜, 暗い間にルール違反をする選手もいた.　　[broke the rules]

   _____

3. 1919年以前は, トップの選手は緑のアームバンドを着けていた.
   　　　　　　　　　　　　　　　　　　[wore a green armband]

   _____

4. 世界中から集まった選手が昨年のレースに出場した.　　[competed in]

   _____

5. 何百万人もの人がスペインやフランスからレースを見に行った.　　[went to watch]

   _____

Guided Practice

自分で言葉を補って英文を完成させましょう.

1. A popular spectator sport in Japan is _____.

2. At school I played _____.

3. At school I never played _____.

4. When we had sports class at school, we wore _____.

5. Last year, the most famous sports star in Japan was _____.

Open Practice

この Unit で学習した文法（動詞の過去形）を使って, 質問に答えましょう.

1. Which sports did you play when you were a child?

   _____

2. Which team sports did you watch on TV last year?

   _____

3. In the last Olympic Games, what sports did you watch?

   _____

UNIT 10

Clean Water

現在完了

Overview

きれいな水がなければ生命は存在することができません．この Unit は脅威にさらされている世界の水についてです．現在完了時制の使われ方に注意しながら，本文を読んでみましょう．

Text　DL 20　CD 20

　　Life on earth **has always needed** clean water to survive. But climate change and pollution **have put** our water supplies at risk and many experts think we are slowly moving towards a global water crisis.

　　They say that climate change **has led** to more violent and frequent
5 storms. Consequently, some areas **have experienced** heavy floods while others suffer from drought. Other changes connected to climate change and water include the melting of the earth's polar ice, rising sea levels and damage to fishing grounds.

　　But it is not only climate change which **has endangered** the safety
10 of our water supplies. Polluted water is a big health risk and continues to threaten our quality of life. Before reaching our lakes and rivers, rainwater often **has picked up** harmful chemicals from farms and factories as well as trash and disease-carrying organisms.

　　Of course, some people **have said** that the experts are exaggerating.
15 They claim that the effects of climate change and pollution on water **have not yet been proved**. But is it really worth the risk and what will happen to humanity if the experts are right?

Glossary

at risk「危機にひんして」　a crisis「危機」　drought「干ばつ」　to endanger「危険にさらす」
a disease-carrying organism「病気を媒介する微生物」　to exaggerate「誇張する，大げさに言う」

UNIT 10 *Clean Water*

Understanding

英文の内容に関する答えとして正しいものを a～c の中から選びましょう．

1. What is the best title for the article?
   a. So Clean
   b. Climate Change
   c. Water at Risk
2. Which two things are the main threats to water supplies?
   a. climate change and pollution
   b. chemicals and rain
   c. storms and drought
3. Which of the following is not connected to climate change?
   a. dangerous chemicals
   b. rising sea levels
   c. melting ice
4. What is one cause of water pollution?
   a. flooding
   b. rising sea levels
   c. farming
5. What do some people think the experts are doing?
   a. polluting water
   b. exaggerating
   c. making money

Collocation Finder DL 21 CD 21

下の囲みの中の語を使って，英文中で使われているコロケーションを完成させましょう．

| heavy | at | on | harmful | quality | violent |

1. _____ risk
2. a _____ flood 
3. _____ of life 
4. a _____ storm 
5. _____ chemicals 
6. _____ earth 

39

Grammar Watch — 現在完了

過去に起きた出来事でも，現在になんらかの影響を及ぼしているときに現在完了という時制を使います．現在完了は「have/has + 過去分詞」という形をしています．過去分詞には過去形と同様，動詞に -ed をつけたものと，不規則変化がありますから，辞書で確認しましょう．

現在完了には大きく分けて 3 つの用法があり，どの用法も「現時点」に基準が置かれます．

- **経験**：「（これまでに）～したことがある」ever, never, once, twice などと共に使い，これまでにしたことがある / ない / 何回した…など「現時点」での経験を語る．
  - 例▶ I **have** never **seen** a ghost.（私はお化けを見たことがない．）
- **完了**：「（今までに）～してしまった」already, not yet, just などと共に使い，すでに「現時点」までにやり終えたこと，まだやっていないこと，ちょうどやり終えたことなどを話すのに用いる．
  - 例▶ I've already **done** my homework.（私はもう宿題を終わらせた．）
- **継続**：「（これまでずっと）～してきた」since, for などと共に用い，ある時点から，またはある期間，「現時点」まで継続して行っていることを言い表す．
  - 例▶ I've **been** sick in bed **since** last weekend.（先週末から病気で寝込んでいる．）

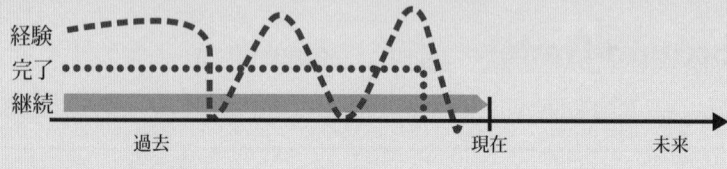

Grammar Try Out

日本語の意味に合うように以下の語句を並べ替え，英文を完成させましょう．

1. 気候変動によって水の安全性が危ぶまれている．
   (has / climate change / safety of / our water / endangered the)

2. 気候の変動により，洪水と干ばつの両方が引き起こされてきた．
   (has / climate change / floods and droughts / caused both)

3. 汚染された水は湖や川にまで到達した．
   (reached our / polluted water / lakes and rivers / has)

4. 専門家は汚水は人の健康にとって大きなリスクであると主張してきた．
   (have said / health risk / is a big / experts / that dirty water)

5. 専門家は誇張しすぎだという人もいた．
   (some / are exaggerating / claimed that / the experts / people have)

UNIT 10 | *Clean Water*

Checkpoint

[ ] 内のキーフレーズを使って日本語に合う英文を作りましょう.

1. 私たちの生活に欠かせないきれいな水が危険にさらされている. [at risk]

_____

2. 汚染のせいで, 水の安全な供給が脅かされている. [has endangered]

_____

3. 水は病気を媒介する微生物を含んでいることがある. [can contain]

_____

4. 有害な化学物質が農場や工場からやってくる. [farms and factories]

_____

5. きれいな水がなかったら, 人類はどうなってしまうのでしょう?
[what would happen]

_____

Guided Practice

自分で言葉を補って英文を完成させましょう.

1. We need clean water to _____.

2. Climate change has led to _____.

3. Polluted water has caused _____.

4. Violent storms have _____.

5. One effect of climate change is _____.

Open Practice

この Unit で学習した文法（現在完了時制）を使って, 質問に答えましょう.

1. Have you ever done anything to protect the environment? What?

_____

2. Have you ever worried about the water in your home? Why?

_____

3. Have you ever thought that the climate change experts might be wrong? Why?

_____

41

UNIT 11

Women in Work

過去形と現在完了形

Overview

仕事は日々の生活の大きな部分を占めます．この Unit はこの 50 年間に女性の就労の機会がどのように改善されてきたかについてです．過去形と現在完了形の使い方に特に注意しながら，以下の文章を読みましょう．

Text DL 22 CD 22

Has your taxi driver ever been a woman? **Have you ever seen** a female doctor? Does your mother work? Does your sister look forward to having a career?

Over the last fifty years there **have been** huge changes in the world of work. Perhaps most notably, in many countries career opportunities for men and women **have become** much more equal.

Fifty years ago many women **stayed** at home, but gradually they **began** to enter the workforce. In the UK in 1971 only 53% of women **worked**, but times **have changed** since then and now over 65% of women are in paid employment.

Attitudes **have changed** too. In 1989, 32% of British men **thought** that they should be the breadwinners and their wives should take care of the home. However, by 2008 only 17% of men **held** this opinion.

But even now we cannot claim that men and women enjoy exactly equal opportunities. Around the world, women are still more likely to be in low-paid jobs and they find it particularly difficult to get promoted to senior positions.

So while women **have made** significant progress in recent years, it seems that there is still plenty of work to do!

Glossary

notably「特に，著しく」 a career opportunity「就業の機会」 the workforce「労働力」
an attitude「意見，考え方」 a breadwinner「一家の大黒柱」 a senior position「上の地位，上級職」

UNIT 11 *Women in Work*

Understanding

英文の内容に関する答えとして正しいものを a ～ c の中から選びましょう．

1. What is the main topic of the article?
   a. more women work   b. women's jobs   c. women in the UK
2. How many women in the UK are now in work?
   a. a minority   b. less than half   c. almost two-thirds
3. By 2008, how many men thought women should take care of the home?
   a. 17%   b. 32%   c. 65%
4. Do women now enjoy equal career opportunities?
   a. yes   b. only in the UK   c. not really
5. What can still be a problem for working women?
   a. getting an education   b. getting promoted   c. finding a job

Collocation Finder DL 23 CD 23

下の囲みの中の語を使って，英文中で使われているコロケーションを完成させましょう．

> hold   paid   stay   particularly   significant   equal

1. _____ opportunities
2. _____ employment 
3. _____ progress 
4. _____ at home 
5. _____ an opinion 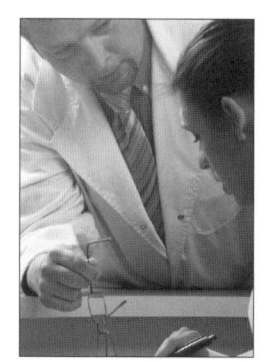
6. _____ difficult 

43

Grammar Watch　過去形と現在完了形

Unit 9 と Unit10 ではそれぞれ過去形と現在完了形について学びました．この 2 つの時制は共に今より前のことを言い表すためのものですが，過去形は単に過去の一時点に起きたことを述べるときに，現在完了は今とのつながりの中で過去の出来事を言い表すのに使います．この Unit ではどのように使い分けるのか，見てみましょう．

- 特定の日時を明記する場合は過去形を，期間やある時点以来と言うときは現在完了を使う．

  例▶ **I met** my boyfriend three years ago.（3 年前という一時点を明記）
  I've known my boyfriend for three years.（3 年間という期間を表す）
  （彼と出会って 3 年になります．）
  ＊I've met my boyfriend three years ago. とは言えない．

- 過去の出来事を過去形でいうときにはその後どうなったかは不明だが，現在完了で言うとその結果が今も続いている（影響している）ことを意味する．

  例▶ **I lost** my watch.（過去の一時点で時計をなくしたが，今も失われた状態かどうかは不明）
  I've lost my watch.（過去の一時点で時計をなくし，現在も見つかっていない．）
  （時計をなくした．）
  ＊I've lost my watch, but I found it later. とは言えない．

Grammar Try Out

日本語の意味に合うように以下の語句を並べ替え，英文を完成させましょう．

1. 女性のタクシー運転手をよく見かける．
   (seen / taxi drivers / many female / I have)

2. 50 年前は 50%近くの女性が，専業主婦だった．
   (of women / ago almost 50% / fifty years / stayed at home)

3. 男性と女性が以前よりずっと平等になった国は多い．
   (and women / in many / countries men / much more equal / have become)

4. 1989 年当時は女性が一家の稼ぎ頭であるべきではないと考えるイギリス人男性が多かった．
   (British men / in 1989 many / breadwinners / thought women / should not be)

5. 女性が給料のいい仕事を得るのは特に難しいのが現状だ．
   (particularly difficult / found it / to get / women have / well-paid jobs)

UNIT 11 | *Women in Work*

Checkpoint

[　] 内のキーフレーズを使って日本語に合う英文を作りましょう．

1. 労働社会は大きく変化した．　　[the world of work]

　_____

2. 近年社会に出て働く女性が多くなった．　　[have entered]

　_____

3. 機会均等に関しては顕著な進歩を遂げてきた．　　[has been made]

　_____

4. 女性が上級職に就くのは難しいと女性達は認識している．　　[senior positions]

　_____

5. 2008年になっても，女性は家にいるべきだと考えるイギリス人男性はまだいた．
　　　　　　　　　　　　　　　　　　　　　　　[should stay at home]

　_____

Guided Practice

自分で言葉を補って英文を完成させましょう．

1. I have thought about becoming a _____.

2. I think career women _____.

3. Fifty years ago in Japan, most women _____.

4. Attitudes in Japan about women working have _____.

5. Before she was married, my mother _____.

Open Practice

この Unit で学習した文法（過去形・現在完了形）を使って，質問に答えましょう．

1. What paid jobs have you done?

　_____

2. Did you do any paid work last year? What was it?

　_____

3. What ambitions do you have for your career?

　_____

45

UNIT 12

Controversy

句動詞

Overview

イギリスでは10年ほど前に公共の場での喫煙が禁止されました．このUnitはこのところ人気を増している電子たばこについてです．句動詞に特に注意をして，次の文章を読んでみましょう．

Text DL 24 CD 24

About a decade after a ban on smoking in public places was introduced, roughly a million people in the UK are now using electronic cigarettes.

Using electronic cigarettes, or e-cigarettes, is called "vaping" because they work by vaporizing liquid nicotine. There's no tobacco and no smoke.
5 It's the smoke in normal cigarettes that kills.

Supporters of e-cigarettes **point out** that what looks like smoke is mostly harmless water vapor. They add that e-cigarettes are great for people who are trying **to give up** smoking and could save tens of thousands of lives.

10 But others don't think they should have **to put up with** e-cigarettes in public places. They are concerned about the health risks connected with their long-term use. They are also worried that children might think e-cigarettes look cool and start using them.

So should people be allowed **to carry on** "vaping" in public? Airlines
15 and train companies say no, as does the University of London, which **brought in** a ban last month. However, with some stores, offices and restaurants allowing them, it seems that this lively controversy will continue for some time yet.

Glossary

a decade「10年間」 a ban「禁止（名詞），禁止する（動詞）」
an electronic cigarette「電子たばこ」 nicotine「ニコチン」
vapor / to vaporize「蒸気／蒸発させる」 a controversy「論争・議論」

UNIT 12 Controversy

Understanding

英文の内容に関する答えとして正しいものを a ～ c の中から選びましょう.

1. How many people in the UK are using e-cigarettes?
   a. more than a million   b. about a million   c. less than a million
2. How much tobacco do e-cigarettes contain?
   a. none   b. a little   c. a lot
3. Why do some people support the use of e-cigarettes?
   a. They are cheap.   b. They help people quit smoking.
   c. They look cool.
4. What worries people who are against e-cigarettes?
   a. the price   b. the water vapor
   c. children might use them
5. What have e-cigarettes caused?
   a. a controversy   b. a total ban   c. health problems

Collocation Finder DL 25 CD 25

下の囲みの中の語を使って, 英文中で使われているコロケーションを完成させましょう.

vapor   health   lively   in   introduce   give up

1. to _____ smoking
2. water _____ 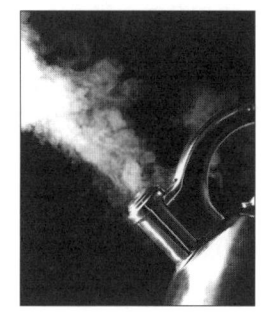
3. a _____ controversy 
4. _____ public 
5. _____ risks 
6. to _____ a ban 

47

Grammar Watch　句動詞

　句動詞というのは，動詞と前置詞や副詞などが組み合わさって，一つの動詞のような意味をなす句のことです（point out「指摘する」, give up ~ing「～することをあきらめる」, put up with「～を我慢する，容認する」など）．
　句動詞と同じ意味を1語で表す動詞もありますが，たいていの場合，1語の難しい語のほうが，句動詞を使うより，堅苦しいイメージになりますので，特に話し言葉では句動詞が多用されます．

例▶ bring in=introduce, carry on=continue, take part in=participate, put up with=endure

ちょうど日本語で「送出する」「結合する」というより，「送り出す」「結びつける」と言った方がくだけた印象になるのと同じでしょう．2語からなるものもあれば，3語以上のものもあります．

例▶ 2語：bring up, hope for, listen to, look at, look for, come across
　　　3語：take care of, get rid of, look forward to, come up with, look up to, make use of

　句動詞を用いれば，ごく一般的な動詞や前置詞などの組み合わせで，たくさんの意味を表すことができるので便利ですが，語の組み合わせを見ただけでは意味が予測できないものもありますから，辞書の成句の欄を活用して，どんどん覚えていきましょう．

Grammar Try Out

日本語の意味に合うように以下の語句を並べ替え，英文を完成させましょう．

1. 水蒸気は無害だと指摘する人もいる．
   (some people / out that / is harmless / point / water vapor)

2. 禁煙するのはとても難しい．
   (it is / smoking / up / very difficult / to give)

3. 公共の場での喫煙を容認しない人はたくさんいる．
   (smoking in public / to put / don't want / many people / up with)

4. 電子たばこを禁止した会社もある．
   (have brought / on e-cigarettes / in a ban / some companies)

5. まだまだこの論争は続きそうだ．
   (on for / will carry / some time yet / the controversy)

UNIT 12 | *Controversy*

Checkpoint

[　]内のキーフレーズを使って日本語に合う英文を作りましょう.

1. イギリスでは，公共の場での喫煙は禁じられている． [public places]

   _____

2. 電子たばこが命を救うと考える人もいる． [save lives]

   _____

3. 電子たばこには，通常のたばこと同様にニコチンが含まれている．
   [contain nicotine]

   _____

4. 電子たばこは水蒸気を発生させるが，煙は出ない． [produce water vapor]

   _____

5. 子供が電子たばこを使い始めるのではないかと心配する人もいる． [start using]

   _____

Guided Practice

自分で言葉を補って英文を完成させましょう．

1. I think that smoking in public is _____.

2. I think that e-cigarettes are _____.

3. I would like to bring in a ban on _____.

4. I worry about the health risks of _____.

5. One controversial subject in Japan is _____.

Open Practice

この Unit で学習した文法（句動詞）を使って，質問に答えましょう．

1. What is your opinion about using e-cigarettes in public places?

   _____

2. What do you find difficult to put up with?

   _____

3. Is there anything you would like to give up?

   _____

49

UNIT 13 The Millennial Generation

未来を表す be going to と will

Overview

20世紀終わり頃に産まれた世代は2000年世代と呼ばれています．このUnitではこの2000年世代が人生に求めるものは何か見ていきます．未来を表すbe going toとwillに注意しながら，次の文章を読みましょう．

Text DL 26 CD 26

　　　If you were born between 1981 and 1998 you are a millennial and by 2025 your generation **will** be 75% of the global workforce. So, what is this generation like and how **is** it **going to** change society? A recent global survey of millennials provided some valuable information.

5　　Millennials want to be leaders. One in four said that they **are going to** be senior managers and want the chance to develop their leadership skills.

　　　Millennials think they **are going to** improve society. 63% of those surveyed give to charities and 43% are actively involved in volunteer work.

　　　Millennials **will** go their own way. Roughly 70% say they **are going to**
10 work independently at some point in the future rather than being employed by a traditional company.

　　　Millennials want to be innovative. Most say that they are interested in creative thinking and **will** choose to work for innovative organisations.

　　　Millennials **will** protect the environment. They believe climate change
15 is real and man-made. 71% support renewable energy like wind and solar and 66% of millennials say they recycle.

Glossary

global workforce「世界の労働人口」　a charity「慈善事業，チャリティ」
actively involved「積極的に関わる」　innovative「革新的な」
man-made「人工の，人によって作られた」　renewable energy「再生可能エネルギー」

UNIT 13 | *The Millennial Generation*

Understanding

英文の内容に関する答えとして正しいものを a 〜 c の中から選びましょう.

1. What is the best title for the article?
   a. The Future   b. The Lazy Generation   c. Millennial Plans
2. Which word best describes the survey of millennials?
   a. international   b. Asian   c. workers
3. What percentage of millennials want to be leaders?
   a. 20%   b. 25%   c. 30%
4. Which subject is not mentioned in the article?
   a. careers   b. green issues   c. family life
5. What do the majority of millennials do?
   a. recycle   b. manage a company   c. volunteer work

Collocation Finder DL 27 CD 27

下の囲みの中の語を使って, 英文中で使われているコロケーションを完成させましょう.

| protect | in | valuable | creative | renewable | give |

1. _____ thinking

2. to _____ to charity

3. _____ energy

4. interested _____ (something)

5. _____ information

6. to _____ the environment

51

Grammar Watch　未来を表す be going to と will

未来の予測，予定，意思などを表すときに be going to や will を使います．どちらも未来のことを表す表現ですが，どのように使い分けたらいいのでしょうか？

- 未来において起きることを単純に述べる場合は will を使います．時間の経過とともに，そのときが来れば起きるであろう未来の事実を表します．

  例▶ It **will** snow tomorrow.（明日は雪になるでしょう．）

- will は強い意志表明にも使えます．上記の単純な未来を表す will と違って，will の部分が強く発音されることが多いです．

  例▶ I **won't** (=will not) give up.（絶対にあきらめないぞ．）
  　　We **will** definitely keep in touch.（絶対連絡取り合いましょうね．）

- 主語がするつもりであるという予定は be going to を使います．これは会話で頻繁に使われ，going to の部分は gonna（「ガナ」のように聞こえる）と短く発音されます．

  例▶ **I'm going to** study abroad next year.（来年留学するつもりです．）

  この表現はあらかじめ考えられていた意志を表しますので，話しているその場で即決した未来の行動には使えません．その場合は will を使います．

  例▶ I'll get it.〈電話が鳴っているのを聞いて〉（私が出るわ．）
  　　＊I'm going to get it. とは言わない．

Grammar Try Out

日本語の意味に合うように以下の語句を並べ替え，英文を完成させましょう．

1. 2000 年世代は 2025 年までに労働人口の大多数を占めることになる．
   (will / millennials / be a majority / workforce by 2025 / of the)

2. 2000 年世代は，自分がリーダーになると言っている．
   (be leaders / say they / millennials / are going to)

3. 2000 年世代は気候変動を信じ，環境保護に努める．
   (protect the environment / climate change and they / millennials believe in / are going to)

4. 多くの 2000 年世代は将来独立して働きたいと思っている．
   (work for / many millennials / will / the future / themselves in)

5. 2000 年世代は革新的な会社で働くことを好む．
   (to work for / innovative companies / will prefer / millennials)

UNIT 13 | *The Millennial Generation*

Checkpoint

[　] 内のキーフレーズを使って日本語に合う英文を作りましょう．

1. 2000年世代は1981年から1998年の間に産まれた．　　[**were born**]

　_____

2. 2000年世代は環境保護に積極的に関わる．　　[**actively involved**]

　_____

3. 2000年世代の63%は慈善事業に寄付をしている．　　[**give to charity**]

　_____

4. 2000年世代は独創的思考と革新的会社に興味がある．　　[**are interested in**]

　_____

5. 2000年世代は従来型の会社に勤めることにあまり興味を持っていない．
　　　　　　　　　　　　　　　　　　　　　　[**traditional companies**]

　_____

Guided Practice

自分で言葉を補って英文を完成させましょう．

1. In my life, I want the chance to _____.

2. This summer, I'm going to _____.

3. Next year, I will _____.

4. I'm going to work for _____.

5. I think the millennial generation will _____.

Open Practice

このUnitで学習した文法（未来を表すbe going toとwill）を使って，質問に答えましょう．

1. Are you going to be a leader in the future?

　_____

2. Do you think your generation will improve society? How?

　_____

3. What kind of work are you going to do?

　_____

UNIT 14 The Key to Long Life

能力・可能性の can と could

Overview

人は健康で長生きすることを望むものです．この Unit は，趣味などに興味を持つことや人と交流することが，長寿の助けになり得るという研究についてです．can, could, be able to の使い方に特に注意しながら，次の文章を読んでみましょう．

Text   DL 28   CD 28

What **can** you do to help yourself live longer? Everyone knows that you shouldn't smoke and it's no surprise that exercise and diet also affect lifespan. However, according to psychologists in Sweden, having interests and a good social life **can** also add years to your life.

5　Following more than 2,000 people over 18 years, researchers found that pursuing interests such as gardening, hiking, going to concerts, cooking and volunteer work **could** extend your life by up to five years.

But having interests is not enough. **Being able to** enjoy them with others was also found to be very important. The researchers discovered
10　that those who lived longest had lots of friends and other people to interact with. In other words, we **could** all benefit from having a good social life and regularly attending social events.

The study shows that we **are** all **able to** influence our lifespan. And living longer doesn't only mean giving up your favorite food or getting up
15　early to go jogging. You **can** also help yourself by enjoying your interests and hanging out with your friends.

Glossary

lifespan「寿命」　according to「〜によると」　a psychologist「心理学者」　a researcher「研究者」
to extend「延ばす」　to interact「交流する」

UNIT 14 *The Key to Long Life*

Understanding

英文の内容に関する答えとして正しいものを a～c の中から選びましょう.

1. Which title would be best for the article?
   a. Don't Smoke
   b. Friends for Life
   c. Give It Up
2. What isn't mentioned in the article?
   a. exercise
   b. illness
   c. food
3. By how many years might having interests lengthen your life?
   a. a maximum of five
   b. a minimum of five
   c. more than five
4. According to paragraph three, what do you need in addition to interests?
   a. regular exercise
   b. money
   c. other people
5. According to the article, who is able to influence how long you live?
   a. yourself
   b. a researcher
   c. your family

Collocation Finder DL 29 CD 29

下の囲みの中の語を使って, 英文中で使われているコロケーションを完成させましょう.

regularly   longer   life   extend   with   interest

1. a social _____
2. pursue an _____ 
3. to _____ attend 
4. to _____ life 
5. to interact _____ 
6. to live _____

Grammar Watch　能力・可能性の can, could

　can には「～することができる」という能力を表す意味があり，is/are able to も同じ意味で用いられます．能力の can を使うと，人があることをできるかできないか，能力に直接言及することになるので，使用を避け，一般動詞で言うことも多いです．また，can には，この意味の他に「～し得る，あり得る」という可能性を表す意味があります．

例▶ ［能力］I **can** handle it.（自分で対処できるよ.）
　　　［能力］**Do**（=**Can**）you speak English?（英語が話せますか?）
　　　［能力］The baby **is able to** walk already.（その赤ちゃんはもう歩ける.）
　　　［可能性］**Can** it be true?（そんなことがあり得るだろうか?）

　could は can の過去形ですが，能力の意味で使われることは少なく，可能性を表す場合によく使われます．その場合，could は can よりさらに低い可能性を表します．「～することができた」という場合は was/were able to を使うのが一般的ですが，could を使うときは通常過去の一時点とわかる語句と共に使われます．

例▶ ［可能性］This **could** be the last chance.（これが最後のチャンスかもね.）
　　　［能力］I **could** run fast when I was a child.（子供の頃は足が速かった.）
　　　［能力］At that time, I **was** still **able to** read without glasses.（あの頃はまだメガネなしで読めた.）

Grammar Try Out

日本語の意味に合うように以下の語句を並べ替え，英文を完成させましょう．

1. 心理学者によると，人は自分の寿命に影響を及ぼすことができるそうだ．
(according to / influence our lifespan / are able to / psychologists, we)

2. いろんなことに興味を持つことが，寿命を5年延ばすことに役立つ可能性がある．
(lot of / live five years longer / help you / interests could / having a)

3. ハイキングや料理などに興味を持つことで，だれもが得することができる．
(interests like / benefit from / everyone can / hiking and cooking)

4. 自分が興味を持っていることを友達と一緒に楽しめることが重要です．
(with friends is / being able / your interests / to enjoy / very important)

5. 友達付き合いをすることが，自分の長生きに役立つのです．
(live longer / you can / by hanging out / help yourself to / with your friends)

UNIT 14 *The Key to Long Life*

Checkpoint

[ ] 内のキーフレーズを使って日本語に合う英文を作りましょう．

1. 運動と食事が寿命に影響することはだれもが知っている．　　[affect lifespan]

___

2. 友達とコンサートに行くなどの活動が自分の役に立つかもしれない．　　[could benefit from]

___

3. たくさんの人と交流することがとても大事だ．　　[interacting with]

___

4. 社交的な人の方が長生きできると研究者は考えている．　　[sociable people]

___

5. 誰しも自分の寿命に影響を及ぼすことができる．　　[how long we live]

___

Guided Practice

自分で言葉を補って英文を完成させましょう．

1. I could benefit from pursuing an interest such as _____.

2. An interest you can pursue in summer is _____.

3. A social event I attend regularly is _____.

4. I think people could live longer if they _____.

5. Interests my friends pursue include _____.

Open Practice

この Unit で学習した文法（能力・可能性の can, could）を使って，質問に答えましょう．

1. What new social events could you participate in?

___

2. Where can you meet new friends?

___

3. How often are you able to hang out with your friends?

___

57

UNIT 15 The Future of Tourism

推量の may と might

Overview

最近では海外で休暇を過ごすのが当たり前になっている人も多いでしょう．この Unit では未来の旅行事情はどうなっているだろうか問いかけています．まずは may と might の使い方に注意しながら，次の文章を読んでみましょう．

Text DL 30 CD 30

　　Planning a vacation? Do you see yourself sunbathing and taking it easy on a beautiful beach or sightseeing in one of Europe's historic cities? These days many people can afford to fly anywhere in the world. But what will the tourism industry of the future look like? Here are three possible scenarios.

5　　People **might** choose to stay at home. Climate change, war and social unrest **might** make traveling overseas more difficult. If this is the future, people **may** choose to take their vacations closer to home.

　　Travel **may** once again become only for the rich. High oil prices and an energy crisis **might** make travel too expensive for ordinary people. In
10 this scenario, only the wealthiest will still be able to take their vacations overseas.

　　Travel **may** become even cheaper and easier. If the global economy improves and technology makes airplanes more fuel-efficient, travel **might** continue getting cheaper and easier. But many popular places will become
15 overcrowded.

　　Of course, no one knows the future. What **might** really happen could be one of these scenarios or something totally different. What do you think?

Glossary
to afford to 「～する（経済的）余裕がある」　a scenario 「シナリオ，筋書き」
social unrest 「（暴動など）社会不安」　an energy crisis 「エネルギー危機」
fuel-efficient 「燃費のよい」　overcrowded 「混雑しすぎる，すし詰め状態の」

UNIT 15　*The Future of Tourism*

Understanding

英文の内容に関する答えとして正しいものを a〜c の中から選びましょう.

1. What is implied about flying in the first paragraph?
   a. It is dangerous.　**b.** It is not expensive.　**c.** It pollutes the air.
2. What possible effect of climate change is mentioned?
   a. more beautiful beaches
   b. an energy crisis
   c. difficult to travel overseas
3. Why might ordinary people stop traveling overseas?
   a. too costly　　　**b.** too dangerous　　　**c.** too easy
4. What might help make overseas travel cheaper?
   a. economic crisis　**b.** overcrowding　　　**c.** technology
5. What does the writer think will happen?
   a. the first scenario
   b. a combination of scenarios
   c. he / she doesn't say

Collocation Finder　DL 31　CD 31

下の囲みの中の語を使って, 英文中で使われているコロケーションを完成させましょう.

> historic　　on　　global　　climate　　take　　tourism

1. to _____ a vacation
2. a _____ city 
3. _____ change 
4. _____ the beach 
5. the _____ economy 
6. the _____ industry

Grammar Watch   推量の may と might

　Unit 13 では未来を表す will, be going to を学びましたが，この Unit では不確定な未来や現在の推量を表す may と might について説明します．両方とも「〜かもしれない」という話者の確信度の低い推量で，どちらかというと might の方が may より可能性が低いものに使われ，「ひょっとしたら」という言葉を添えるとぴったりします．しかし，可能性の差はなく用いられることも多いようです．

例▶ At first glance, you **may** not notice any differences.（一目では違いがわからないかもしれない．）
My son **might** become famous in the future.（ひょっしたら息子は有名になるかもしれない．）

may は許可「〜してもよい」という意味もありますが，might には推量の意味しかありません．

例▶ You **may** go home now.（もう帰ってよろしい．）
Jane **may** be home by now.（ジェーンはもう家に帰ってるかも．）
You **might** be home within an hour.（1 時間以内にうちに着いてるかもね．）

「〜できるようになるかもしれない」のように可能と推量の意味を組み合わせたいときには，can と may や might を同時に使うことはできませんが，may や might と be able to を組み合わせて使うことができます．

例▶ You **may/might** be able to help her.（あなたなら彼女を救えるかもしれない．）

Grammar Try Out

日本語の意味に合うように以下の語句を並べ替え，英文を完成させましょう．

1. 気候変動のために，人は旅行をしなくなるかもしれない．
(may stop / of climate change / travelling because / people)

2. 社会不安のせいで，人は出かけなくなるかもしれない．
(social unrest / at home / might / to stay / cause people)

3. お金持ちしか飛行機で海外旅行に行けなくなるかもしれない．
(be able to / rich may / only the / fly overseas)

4. エネルギー効率のいい飛行機ができたら，旅行はもっと安くなるかもしれない．
(airplanes might / fuel efficient / travel cheaper / make)

5. 未来の旅行事情はこれらのシナリオとは全く異なるかもしれない．
(completely different / tourism in the / from these scenarios / future might be)

UNIT 15 *The Future of Tourism*

Checkpoint

[　] 内のキーフレーズを使って日本語に合う英文を作りましょう.

1. 私がきれいなビーチでくつろいでいるのが目に浮かびます. [see myself]

_____

2. 次の休暇には歴史的な街を訪れるかもしれません. [a historic city]

_____

3. 石油価格の高騰で, 航空運賃はもっと高くなるかもしれません.
[become more expensive]

_____

4. 世界経済が改善したら旅行はもっと安くなるかもしれない.
[the global economy]

_____

5. もっと安く旅行できるようになれば, あちこちで混雑するでしょう.
[become overcrowded]

_____

Guided Practice

自分で言葉を補って英文を完成させましょう.

1. Tonight, I might _____.

2. This weekend, I may _____.

3. Next spring vacation, I might _____.

4. Next summer, I may _____.

5. I think overseas vacations might become _____.

Open Practice

この Unit で学習した文法（推量の may と might）を使って, 質問に答えましょう

1. Where are you thinking of going on your next vacation?

_____

2. Do you think travel will become cheaper or more expensive? Why?

_____

3. How do you think tourism will change in the future?

_____

61

UNIT 16

Cheaper Travel

義務・必要を表す should と must

Overview

電車の運賃がお得になるに越したことはないですよね．この Unit は割引切符を買うための Railcard の使い方についてです．助動詞 should, must の使い方に注意しながら，次の文章を読んでみましょう．

Text DL 32 CD 32

Thank you for choosing the Friends Railcard. Before using your new Railcard, please read the following terms and conditions.

1. You **must** sign your Railcard before use to show that you accept all of the terms and conditions.
2. Tickets bought with your Railcard **must not** be given, loaned, or resold to anyone else. Only you can use your Railcard.
3. You **must** travel with at least one other person to enable discount tickets to be used.
4. Tickets for your journey **should** be purchased before boarding the train and when buying tickets you **must** show your Railcard.
5. You **should** carry your Railcard with you on your journey and when asked by rail staff you **must** show both a valid ticket and valid Railcard.
6. If your Railcard is damaged, lost or stolen, you **should** apply for a replacement online.

And don't forget that your Railcard gives you more than cheap travel! You can also get huge discounts when you are on vacation, eating out and much more! Visit our website to keep up to date with all the latest discounts!

Glossary

terms and conditions「利用規約」 to accept「（規約など）を受け入れる，に同意する」
a discount ticket「割引乗車券」 valid「有効である」 a replacement「交換，再発行」
to eat out「外食する」

UNIT 16 *Cheaper Travel*

Understanding

英文の内容に関する答えとして正しいものを a～c の中から選びましょう．

1. Which item most appropriately describes the article?
   a. a story
   b. an essay
   c. a list
2. What must you do before using your Railcard?
   a. show it
   b. sign it
   c. open it
3. What is the Railcard for?
   a. reserving a seat
   b. buying cheaper tickets
   c. traveling to work
4. When can you use discounted tickets?
   a. when with other people
   b. when alone
   c. when on vacation
5. Where else can you use your Railcard?
   a. at school
   b. on the Internet
   c. in restaurants

Collocation Finder DL 33 CD 33

下の囲みの中の語を使って，英文中で使われているコロケーションを完成させましょう．

| visit | on | huge | valid | for | board |

1. a _____ ticket
2. to _____ a train 
3. to _____ a website 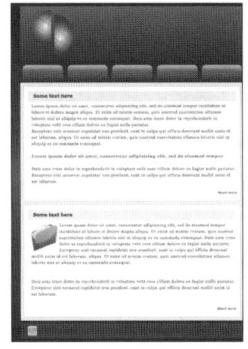
4. a _____ discount 
5. to apply _____ (something) 
6. _____ vacation

Grammar Watch　義務・必要を表す should と must

利用規約など規則を表す文章には「～しなければならない」「～してはいけない」のような利用者の義務や必要を表す表現が多く使われます．最も直接的なのは命令文で言う方法ですが，should や must を使って同じようなことを言い表せます．この際，should より must の方が義務・必要の高い度合いを表します．

例▶ **Show** your ticket.（命令文：切符を見せなさい．）
Don't lend your card.（命令文：カードを他人に貸してはいけません．）
You **should** be careful when crossing the street.（横断歩道を渡るときは注意しなさい．）
You **must** carry your passport all the time.（パスポートは常時携帯しなければならない．）

同じような意味を表すものには，ought to, have to, need to などもあります．

例▶ You **need to** wear a suit to the interview.（面接はスーツ着用のこと．）

否定文で使うときには should not, must not, ought not to は「してはいけない」を表すのに対し，don't have to, need not (to) は「しなくてもよい」を表します．

例▶ You **should not** litter.（ポイ捨てしてはいけません．）
You **don't have to** be perfect.（完璧である必要はありません．）

Grammar Try Out

日本語の意味に合うように以下の語句を並べ替え，英文を完成させましょう．

1. Railcard を他人に貸与することはできません．
   (lend your / you / should not / anyone else / Railcard to)

2. 割引切符を使うには同行者が必要です．
   (travel with / a discount ticket / you must / when using / another person)

3. 割引切符を購入する際は Railcard の提示が必要です．
   (when buying / you / your Railcard / must show / discount tickets)

4. 鉄道職員が求めた場合，乗車券と Railcard の両方を提示してください．
   (rail staff, you / ticket and Railcard / should show / when asked by / both your)

5. Railcard を紛失した際はオンラインで再発行の手続きをとってください．
   (a replacement / lose your Railcard / you should / online if you / apply for)

UNIT 16 | *Cheaper Travel*

Checkpoint

[ ] 内のキーフレーズを使って日本語に合う英文を作りましょう．

1. Railcard を使用する前にすべての利用条件に同意する必要があります．
[the terms and conditions]
_____

2. 名義人以外の者に Railcard を使用した乗車券の購入をさせないでください．
[shouldn't let]
_____

3. 乗車券は旅行開始前にご購入ください．   [purchase a ticket]
_____

4. Railcard を使えば大幅な割引が受けられます．   [a huge discount]
_____

5. 旅行中は有効な乗車券を必ずお持ちください．   [a valid ticket]
_____

Guided Practice

自分で言葉を補って文を完成させましょう．

1. I should take a trip to visit _____.

2. I must not forget to _____.

3. When boarding a train, people should _____.

4. Train passengers must make sure they _____.

5. To save money, you should _____.

Open Practice

この Unit で学習した文法（義務・必要を表す should と must）を使って，質問に答えましょう．

1. What should you do tonight?
_____

2. What must you do next weekend?
_____

3. What advice would you give to someone visiting your hometown?
_____

UNIT 17 Word of the Year

Wh- 疑問文

Overview

私たちが使う言葉は時間とともに変化します．このUnitは，オックスフォード英語辞典が毎年どのように流行語大賞を選んでいるのかを説明しています．Wh- 疑問文に注意をしながら，次の文章を読んで見ましょう．

Text DL 34 CD 34

All languages evolve and English is no exception. Read this interview and find out how Oxford Dictionaries celebrates this fact with its Word of the Year award.

What is the Word of the Year award?

It's something we do for fun to show how English changes. As society and technology change, some words become less common while others suddenly become very popular indeed.

When did you start giving this award?

Over ten years ago now. It started in 2004.

How do you choose the Word of the Year?

It's not necessarily a new word, just one which has become popular. We use software to collect and analyze about 150 million words that are used on the web each month.

What is this year's Word of the Year?

It's selfie!

Why did you choose selfie?

Because this year the frequency of selfie, first used in 2002, increased by 17,000%. That's amazing!

How do you define selfie?

We define the word as "a photograph that one has taken of oneself, typically with a smartphone or webcam and uploaded to a social media website."

Glossary

to evolve「発達・進化・発展する」 an exception「例外」 to analyze「分析する」
frequency「頻度」 typically「典型的に，一般的に」 social media「(SNSなどの) ソーシャルメディア」

UNIT 17 *Word of the Year*

Understanding

英文の内容に関する答えとして正しいものを a ～ c の中から選びましょう.

1. Identify the true statement.
   a. English doesn't change.   **b.** English evolves.   **c.** English is different.
2. What can cause a word to suddenly become very popular?
   a. fun   **b.** an award   **c.** social change
3. When did Oxford Dictionaries give the first Word of the Year award?
   a. 2002   **b.** 2004   **c.** ten years ago
4. When was the word 'selfie' first used?
   a. 2002   **b.** 2004   **c.** this year
5. Who can take a selfie of you?
   a. yourself   **b.** a friend   **c.** anyone

Collocation Finder   DL 35   CD 35

下の囲みの中の語を使って，英文中で使われているコロケーションを完成させましょう.

> on   take   out   define   for   give

1. find _____
2. _____ a word 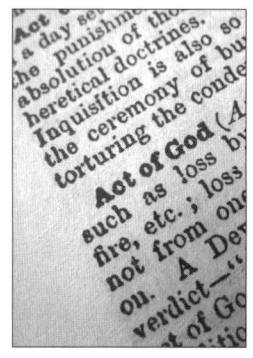
3. _____ the web 
4. _____ a photograph 
5. _____ an award 
6. _____ fun 

67

Grammar Watch — Wh- 疑問文

人からいろんな情報を聞き出すためには質問をします．「いつ」「どこで」「だれと」「どうやって」など知りたい情報を手に入れるためには，それに合った疑問詞を用います．What, Who, Where, When, Why, How という疑問詞は疑問文の先頭に置かれます．

What と Who は疑問文の主語や目的語になる疑問文ですが，特に What には日本人学習者には使いにくいけれど，一般的にはよく使われる用法があります．ものを主語としてそれが何かを引き起こすという「もの主語」の言い方です．

例▶ **What** made you think so?（何があなたにそう思わせたの？→なぜそう思ったの？）
What caused the problem?（何がその問題を引き起こしたの？→原因は何？）

Where, When, Why, How は副詞的な要素を問います．その中でも，手段を問う How が使えると便利です．

例▶ **How** did you get here?（どうやってきたの？→交通手段を聞く．）
How do you manage your time?（時間の使い方を教えて．）

質問は情報をうまく引き出すのに有効なだけではなく，円滑なコミュニケーションにも不可欠です．場面によって的確な質問ができるよう，練習を重ねましょう．

Grammar Try Out

日本語の意味に合うように以下の語句を並べ替え，英文を完成させましょう．

1. 言葉が変化する原因はなんですか?
   (causes / what / change / languages to)

2. 言葉はどのようにして収集・分析されるのですか?
   (analyze words / do they / how / collect and)

3. あの言葉の意味はなんですか?
   (word / is the / of that / what / meaning)

4. selfie という単語の頻度が 17,000% も増えたのはいつですか?
   (did the / 17,000% / increase by / frequency of selfie / when)

5. selfie はなぜ受賞したのですか?
   (did selfie / why / the award / win)

UNIT 17 | *Word of the Year*

Checkpoint

[ ] 内のキーフレーズを使って日本語に合う英文を作りましょう.

1. 言葉がどのようにして変化するのか知りたい.   [**find out**]

   _____

2. ソフトウェアを使って毎月約 1 億 5 千万語が収集される.   [**use software**]

   _____

3. 流行語大賞は 10 年以上前に初めて授与された.   [**was first given**]

   _____

4. 冗談で使う言葉にはどんなものがありますか？   [**for fun**]

   _____

5. 自分撮り画像をどうやってウェブにアップしますか？   [**upload a selfie**]

   _____

Guided Practice

自分で言葉を補って英文を完成させましょう.

1. My favorite word or phrase in English is _____.

2. An English word or phrase I don't like is _____.

3. My favorite popular phrase in Japanese is _____.

4. My Word of the Year in Japanese would be _____.

5. I think selfies are _____.

Open Practice

この Unit で学習した文法（Wh- 疑問文）を使って，自分撮り画像について尋ねる質問を 3 つ書きましょう.

1. What _____?

2. When _____?

3. How _____?

UNIT 18

Considering Others

丁寧な疑問文

Overview

マナーを守ることは人とのコミュニケーションの潤滑油になります．この Unit はお互いの気遣いがもたらす恩恵についてです．助動詞を使った疑問文に注意しながら，次の文章を読んでみましょう．

Text DL 36 CD 36

　　Don't speak with your mouth full. Look people in the eye when you talk to them. Say please when you ask for something. Good manners show consideration for others and are the traffic lights of human interaction, keeping people from crashing into one another in everyday behavior.

5　　And being polite to others also helps when asking for help or information. Are you more or less likely to help someone who treats you with respect and consideration? The answer is obvious.

　　What time is it? How much will it cost? Where is the bathroom? How would those questions make you feel? Spoken to like that, most of us would
10　feel somewhat unappreciated and less willing to help. The questions are too direct. In fact, they are a little rude.

　　Can you tell me what time it is? Do you have any idea how much it will cost? Do you know where the bathroom is? That sounds so much better! Good manners cost nothing, show consideration for others
15　and help you get what you want. They make you, and those around you, feel good. Now, what's not to like about that?

Glossary
consideration「思いやり」　traffic lights「交通信号」　interaction「やりとり」
polite「礼儀正しい，気遣いのある」　unappreciated「感謝されない，ぞんざいに扱われる」
rude「無礼な，失礼な」

UNIT 18 *Considering Others*

Understanding

英文の内容に関する答えとして正しいものを a～c の中から選びましょう．

1. What should you do when talking to people?
   a. keep quiet
   b. say please
   c. make eye contact
2. In what way are good manners like traffic lights?
   a. They prevent accidents.
   b. They stop people.
   c. They show consideration.
3. How might you feel when someone is rude to you?
   a. respected
   b. unappreciated
   c. willing
4. What can sound rude?
   a. being too willing
   b. being too direct
   c. asking questions
5. What is one benefit of good manners?
   a. getting what you want
   b. saving money
   c. being respected

Collocation Finder   DL 37   CD 37

下の囲みの中の語を使って，英文中で使われているコロケーションを完成させましょう．

> into   direct   show   to   human   a little

1. _____ interaction
2. to crash _____ (something) 
3. a _____ question 
4. to _____ consideration 
5. polite _____ (someone) 
6. _____ rude 

71

Grammar Watch　丁寧な疑問文

だれでも丁寧に質問された方が，答えてあげたい気持ちになりますよね．ぶしつけな質問を避けるのは英語でも同じです．元々の疑問文を，Can you tell me~?, Do you know~?, Do you have any idea~? などのもう一つの疑問文で囲ってしまうようにして丁寧な疑問文を作ることができます．

例▶　△ How much is it?（これいくら？）
○ **Can you tell me** how much it is?（いくらか教えてくれます？）

そのとき，元々の疑問文の語順は疑問文のものから，平叙文のものへと戻ります．

例▶　○ **Can you tell me** where I can find the book?
× Can you tell me where can I find the book?

また，元々の疑問文の疑問詞をなくして数語にまとめてしまうこともできます．

例▶　Can you tell me **what time it is**? → Can you tell me **the time**?（何時か教えてくれます？）
Can you tell me **how to get to** City Hall? → Can you tell me the way to City Hall?（市役所へ行く道を教えてくれます？）

can より could を使ったり，please 添えたりした方がより丁寧になりますが，よほどの無理なお願いでない限り，必要以上に丁寧度を増すとよそよそしさを強調することになりかねませんから，ほどほどにしておきましょう．

Grammar Try Out

日本語の意味に合うように以下の語句を並べ替え，英文を完成させましょう．

1. その電車は何時に出るかわかりますか？
   (time the / know what / do you / train leaves)

   _____

2. チケットがいくらか見当がつきますか？
   (any idea / do / a ticket costs / you have / how much)

   _____

3. 最寄りのコンビニはどこか教えてもらえますか？
   (tell me where / can you / the nearest / is / convenience store)

   _____

4. 彼がなぜここに居ないのか知ってますか？
   (why / you know / do / here / he isn't)

   _____

5. 駅に行く道を教えてもらえますか？
   (tell me / can you / get to / how to / the station)

   _____

UNIT 18 | *Considering Others*

Checkpoint

[　] 内のキーフレーズを使って日本語に合う英文を作りましょう.

1. マナーを守るのがなぜ大切なのか教えてもらえますか？　　[good manners]

   _____

2. 自分に敬意を払ってくれる人の方をより助けてあげたい気になるでしょう.
   　　　　　　　　　　　　　　　　　　　　[treats you with respect]

   _____

3. 直接的な質問はちょっと失礼に聞こえる.　　　[can sound]

   _____

4. 彼女がどこにいるか，心当たりありますか？　　[any idea]

   _____

5. マナーを守るとみんなが心地いい.　　[feel good]

   _____

Guided Practice

自分で言葉を補って英文を完成させましょう.

1. I think being polite is important because _____.

2. I think good manners help people to _____.

3. Children should be taught to _____.

4. My mother always told me to _____.

5. When people are impolite I feel _____.

Open Practice

このユニットで学習した文法（丁寧な疑問文）を使って，3つ質問を作りましょう.

1. Can you tell me _____?

2. Do you have any idea _____?

3. Do you know _____?

73

UNIT 19

Healthy Grades

時と場所を表す前置詞

Overview

心の健康と体の健康の間には本当に関連があるのでしょうか．この Unit は運動がティーンエイジャーの学業成績にどのような影響を与えるのかについてです．時や場所を表す前置詞に注意しながら，次の文章を読んでみましょう．

Text　DL 38　CD 38

　People have long thought that there is a link between a healthy body and a healthy mind. **In** Scotland, researchers have produced evidence to suggest that this is probably true, finding that exercise improves the academic performance of teenagers **at** school.

5　　A study of about 5,000 children found a link between physical activity and exam success in English, math and science. Children who did regular exercise not only did better on tests **at** 11, but also **at** 13 and in exams **at** 16.

　The researchers found that just 15 minutes of moderate exercise
10　improved academic performance by about a quarter of a grade. And they claim that children who do one hour of exercise every day could improve their academic performance by a full grade—for example, from a C to a B, or a B to an A.

　Most teenagers don't do an hour of exercise a day, but might this be a
15　valuable lesson for schools? In future perhaps schools should concentrate on performance **on** the playing field as much as they do on performance **in** the classroom. Should they be making students do an hour of sports every day?

Glossary

a link「関連，繋がり，リンク」　academic performance「学業成績」　physical activity「運動」
a quarter「4分の1」　to concentrate「集中する」　the playing field「運動場」

UNIT 19 *Healthy Grades*

Understanding

英文の内容に関する答えとして正しいものを a～c の中から選びましょう．

1. Is the link between a healthy mind and a healthy body a new idea?
   a. yes
   b. no
   c. it isn't mentioned
2. Where was the study of 5,000 children done?
   a. in England
   b. in Scotland
   c. in one school
3. How was academic performance measured by the researchers?
   a. by doing exercise
   b. using a questionnaire
   c. by taking tests
4. How much exercise might improve performance by a grade?
   a. 11 and 13
   b. an hour a day
   c. 15 minutes
5. What might schools learn from the study?
   a. to do more sports
   b. to do fewer tests
   c. to give better tests

Collocation Finder DL 39 CD 39

下の囲みの中の語を使って，英文中で使われているコロケーションを完成させましょう．

concentrate   between   moderate   produce   on   valuable

1. _____ tests
2. a _____ lesson 
3. a link _____ 
4. to _____ on 
5. _____ exercise 
6. to _____ evidence 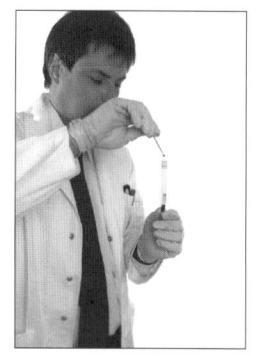

75

Grammar Watch　時と場所を表す前置詞

場所を表す前置詞の基本は at, on, in です．イメージとしては，at はある一地点を，on はある平面の上に乗っている状態を，in はある空間の中を表しますが，なにを点・面・空間と捉えるかは一貫しているようには見えないかもしれません．どんな場所を表す名詞にどんな前置詞が使われるかセットで覚えていきましょう．

例▶ **at** school, **at** university, **at** the station, **at** a restaurant
on the playing ground, **on** a farm, **on** a bus, **on** a plane
in the classroom, **in** (the) hospital, **in** Japan/Kyoto（国名・都市名）

時を表す前置詞も基本は at, on, in です．at (at night) ＜ on (on Sunday) ＜ in (in 2011) の順に一時点からより幅のある時間を表すイメージはありますが，場所を表す前置詞と同様，名詞とセットで覚えるのがいいでしょう．物事の前後関係を表すのには before（〜の前），after（〜の後）も便利です．

例▶ **after** school（放課後），the day **after** tomorrow（明後日）
before the accident（事故の前），the year **before** last（一昨年）

その他にもコロケーションとしてその前に来る名詞や動詞までセットで覚えておくとよい前置詞の使い方もあります（a link **between** 〜 and 〜, do well **on** the test）．前置詞はとても短い語なのに用法が多岐に渡ります．一つずつ確認して身につけましょう．

Grammar Try Out

日本語の意味に合うように以下の語句を並べ替え，英文を完成させましょう．

1. 子供の学校での成績を上げるのはとても大切だ．
   (is very important / children at / academic performance of / improving the / school)

2. 運動をすると授業の成績がよくなる．
   (activity improves / the classroom / performance in / physical)

3. 子供達は 11 歳，13 歳，16 歳で試験を受けた．
   (tests at / the children / 11, 13 / took / and 16)

4. 15 分運動をした後の方が子供達の成績はよかった．
   (the children / of exercise / 15 minutes / tests after / did better on)

5. ティーンエイジャーは運動場にいる時間をもっと増やすべきだ．
   (spend more / teenagers should / time on / field / the playing)

UNIT 19 | *Healthy Grades*

Checkpoint

[　] 内のキーフレーズを使って日本語に合う英文を作りましょう.

1. 研究者は運動と学業成績には関連があると考えている. 　　[a link between]

_____

2. 活発な子供の方が英語, 数学, 理科のテストの点がよかった. 　　[active children]

_____

3. たった 15 分の運動で, 成績が上がった. 　　[academic performance]

_____

4. 毎日運動すると成績を一段階上げられるかもしれない. 　　[could improve]

_____

5. 今後はティーンエイジャーは全員毎日学校で運動をするべきなのかもしれない.
　　　　　　　　　　　　　　　　　　　　　　　　　　　　[should exercise]

_____

Guided Practice

自分で言葉を補って英文を完成させましょう.

1. I think a healthy mind needs _____.

2. I improve my academic performance by _____.

3. I think regular exercise is _____.

4. I keep my body healthy by _____.

5. I think schools should _____.

Open Practice

この Unit で学習した文法（時と場所を表す前置詞）を使って, 質問に答えましょう

1. How much exercise did you do in elementary school?

_____

2. How much exercise did you do in high school?

_____

3. Where and when do you exercise these days?

_____

UNIT 20 A History of the Internet

前置詞 by, during, for

Overview

インターネットはいつからあって，誰が作ったのでしょうか？この Unit ではインターネットがどのように始まって，どうやって発展してきたかを説明します．by, during, for の使い方に注意しながら，次の文章を読んでみましょう．

Text DL 40 CD 40

How old is the Internet and who invented it? We think of the Internet and technologies such as email as modern inventions, so it might surprise you to find out that they have been around **for** over 40 years.

During the Cold War, when the USA and the Soviet Union were fierce
5 rivals, America wanted to develop superior technology. As a result, **by** 1969 it had set up the world's first computer network, allowing huge computers to speak to each other. The history of the Internet had begun and the first email was sent three years later.

For over 20 years the Internet was owned and used exclusively by the
10 United States government. This changed in 1992 when President George Bush allowed it to be used for private and business purposes.

But two other technological innovations were needed to create the Internet we now use. The first was the personal computer (PC), developed **during** the early 1970s. The second was the World Wide Web, invented by
15 Tim Berners-Lee, a British scientist who also created HTML. This had been made available to web authors **by** 1991.

So, to answer our original question, the Internet was not invented by any single individual and has been around for much longer than many of us realize.

Glossary
to be around「ある，存在する」 the Cold War「冷戦」 the Soviet Union「ソビエト連邦」
a rival「ライバル，競争相手」 exclusively「独占的に，まったく〜のみ」
a technological innovation「技術革新」

UNIT 20 | *A History of the Internet*

Understanding

英文の内容に関する答えとして正しいものを a～c の中から選びましょう．

1. When did the history of the Internet begin?
   a. in the 1970s   b. about 20 years ago   c. during the Cold War
2. When was the first email sent?
   a. by 1969   b. about 1972   c. in 1992
3. When could companies first use the Internet?
   a. 1969   b. 1991   c. 1992
4. Where did the creator of HTML come from?
   a. the Soviet Union   b. the UK   c. the USA
5. Who invented the Internet?
   a. George Bush   b. Tim Berners-Lee   c. many different people

Collocation Finder   DL 41   CD 41

下の囲みの中の語を使って，英文中で使われているコロケーションを完成させましょう．

early   modern   fierce   develop   technological   purposes

1. a _____ invention
2. a _____ innovation 
3. business _____ 
4. the _____ 1970s 
5. _____ rivals 
6. to _____ technology 

79

Grammar Watch　　前置詞 by, during, for

duringとforは両方「期間」を表しますが, during は「いつ」物事が起こるか, for はそれが「どれくらい長く」続くかを表します.

例▶ I got sick **during** my stay in London.（ロンドン滞在中に病気になった.）
　　　I stayed in London **for** about a month.（ロンドンには1ヶ月くらい滞在した.）

「期限」の by は「そのときまでにはもう〜していた.」という時に使われますので,多くの場合, 過去完了形（had + 過去分詞）と共に使われます. また, 未来のことを言う場合には, 未来形と共に使われることもあります.

例▶ He had taken refuge in the church **by** then.（そのときは彼はすでに教会に逃げ込んでいた.）

byとuntilはどちらも「〜まで」という日本語で表されるので, 混同しがちですが, by はその時点までには完了していることを示す一方, until はその時点まで継続されていることを示し, 意味が全く異なります.

例▶ I'll be back **by** Friday.（金曜日までには戻るよ.）
　　　I'll be here **until** Friday.（金曜までここに居るよ.）

Grammar Try Out

日本語の意味に合うように以下の語句を並べ替え, 英文を完成させましょう.

1. 冷戦時代, アメリカ合衆国とソ連はライバルだった.
   (during / and the Soviet Union / were rivals / the USA / the Cold War)

   _____

2. メールの送受信は1970年代に始まった.
   (sending and / people started / the 1970s / during / receiving email)

   _____

3. 何年もの間, インターネットは合衆国政府が独占的に使用していた.
   (was used only / years the Internet / of the United States / for many / by the government)

   _____

4. 1990年後半には企業や個人がインターネットを使用するようになっていた.
   (businesses and / the late 1990s / the Internet by / were using / private individuals)

   _____

5. 1991年には, Tim Berners-Lee はすでにウェブとHTMLの両方を作っていた.
   (had created / both the / Tim Berners-Lee / by 1991 / World Wide Web and HTML)

   _____

UNIT 20 *A History of the Internet*

Checkpoint

[　] 内のキーフレーズを使って日本語に合う英文を作りましょう.

1. E メールはもう何十年も存在している.　　[has been around]

___

2. アップルとマイクロソフトは何年もの間, 激しいライバル関係にあった.
[fierce rivals]

___

3. 冷戦のおかげで多くの技術革新が生まれた.　　[technological innovations]

___

4. 1990 年代後半, インターネットの人気に火がつき始めた.　　[the late 1990s]

___

5. 2025 年までにはインターネットは商用目的にのみ使用されるようになるだろう.
[used exclusively]

___

Guided Practice

自分で言葉を補って英文を完成させましょう.

1. During the weekends, I mainly use the Internet for _____.

2. During my time at high school, my favorite computer game was _____
_____.

3. I have to email my friend by _____.

4. I had my own mobile phone by _____.

Open Practice

この Unit で学習した文法（前置詞 by, during, for）を使って, 質問に答えましょう.

1. During your free time, what do you like to do on the Internet?
_____

2. For how many hours a day do you use the Internet?
_____

3. By 2025, how do you think the Internet will have changed?
_____

81

UNIT 21: The Statistics of Safety

手段・方法の by

Overview

飛行機は本当に一番安全な交通手段なのでしょうか？ より安全に旅するにはどうしたらいいのでしょうか．この Unit を読めば答えが分かります．手段・方法を表す前置詞 by の使い方に注意しながら，次の文章を読んでみましょう．

Text DL 42 CD 42

How scared do you feel when an airplane is taking off? It's often said that flying is the safest form of transport, but when an airplane crashes the media coverage can make that hard to believe. However, it is true.

In the United States, the average person's chance of dying in a plane crash is about one in 5,000. In contrast, the chances of being killed in a road accident are about one in 83. And that number also includes those who are on foot, traveling **by** bicycle or riding a motorbike.

Still, flying makes many people somewhat anxious. What can you do to make it as safe as possible? First, fly **by** direct routes to reduce the number of times you take off and land, which is when most accidents occur. Second, **by** paying attention to the preflight briefing you will know where the emergency exits are located. Third, **by** keeping your seatbelt fastened you will avoid injury from unexpected turbulence.

Finally, don't forget the statistics. Because however scared you feel, it should comfort you to know that flying really is the safest form of transport.

Glossary
media coverage 「マスコミの報道」　anxious 「心配な」　a direct route 「直行便」
a preflight briefing 「離陸前のアナウンス」　turbulence 「乱気流」　statistics 「統計」

UNIT 21 | *The Statistics of Safety*

Understanding

英文の内容に関する答えとして正しいものを a 〜 c の中から選びましょう.

1. What can make it hard to believe that flying is safe?
   a. the statistics   b. road accidents   c. stories in the news
2. Is flying safer than traveling by road?
   a. yes   b. no   c. it depends
3. Who is included in road accident statistics?
   a. people in parks   b. people on trains   c. people walking
4. When do most air accidents happen?
   a. on take off and landing b. on direct flights   c. during turbulence
5. Which piece of advice is not given in the article?
   a. fasten your seatbelt   b. sit by an exit   c. take direct flights

Collocation Finder DL 43   CD 43

下の囲みの中の語を使って, 英文中で使われているコロケーションを完成させましょう.

| fasten | in | take | avoid | possible | hard |

1. to _____ off
2. to _____ injury 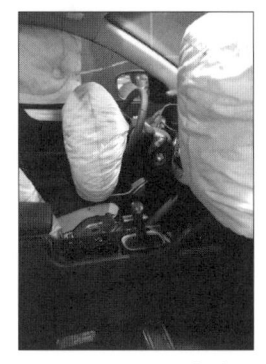
3. to _____ a seatbelt 
4. as safe as _____ 
5. _____ contrast 
6. _____ to believe 

83

Grammar Watch　手段・方法の by

前置詞 by の用法のうち，ここでは手段・方法について学びます．
- 交通手段（例▶ by bus, by train, by car, by plane）．交通手段を表す名詞に a, the などの冠詞は付けません．ただし，「徒歩で」という場合は on foot. となります．
- （情報や荷物などの）伝達・運搬方法（例▶ by email, by fax, by phone, by post）．
- 方法（例▶ pay **by** credit card（クレジットカードで支払う），learn English **by** a new method（新しい方法で英語を学ぶ），write a letter **by** hand（手紙を手書きする）．

「手段」という意味の means と一緒に用いて，by means of ~ というと，by のみの場合よりかしこまった感じになります．

例▶ In this study, data were collected **by means of** interviews and questionnaires.（本研究では，インタビューとアンケートという手段によりデータを収集した．）

by の後に動名詞（動詞 +ing）を続けると「~することによって」と，その方法の具体的な動きを説明することができます．

例▶ The president began his speech **by** celebrat**ing** the treaty signed a day earlier.（大統領は前日の条約締結を祝ってスピーチを始めた．）

Grammar Try Out

日本語の意味に合うように以下の語句を並べ替え，英文を完成させましょう．

1. 飛行機は最も安全な交通手段だと言われています．
(the safest form / traveling by / it's said that / of transport / air is)

___

2. 自動車での移動は飛行機よりもずっと危険です．
(by car / than flying / traveling / is more dangerous)

___

3. 離陸前のアナウンスに注意をして，緊急時にどうするべきか知っておきましょう．
(to the preflight briefing / by / do in an emergency / know what to / paying attention)

___

4. シートベルトを締めて，けがを防ぎましょう．
(seatbelt fastened / by / avoid injury / keeping your)

___

5. 飛行機が最も安全な移動手段だということを念頭に置いて，気を楽にしましょう．
(remembering that flying / to travel / feel better / is the safest way / by)

___

UNIT 21 | *The Statistics of Safety*

Checkpoint

[　] 内のキーフレーズを使って日本語に合う英文を作りましょう．

1. 事故時のマスコミの報道を見ると，飛行機が危険に感じるかもしれません．　　[media coverage]

   _____

2. 路上での交通事故で死亡する確率の方がずっと高いです．　　[road accidents]

   _____

3. このアドバイスに従えば飛行機の旅はより安全になります．

   [following this advice]

   _____

4. 車で移動するときにはいつもシートベルトを締めていますか？　　[seatbelt fastened]

   _____

5. 非常口がどこにあるかしっかり頭に入れておきましょう．　　[emergency exits]

   _____

Guided Practice

自分で言葉を補って英文を完成させましょう．

1. Flying makes me feel _____.

2. I feel safest when I travel _____.

3. When I'm in a car, I _____.

4. Media coverage of accidents makes me _____.

5. I'd advise people on airplanes to _____.

Open Practice

この Unit で学習した文法（手段・方法の by）を使って，質問に答えましょう．

1. Would you fly or take a train if the ticket prices were exactly the same?

   _____

2. What do you do to make your journeys as safe as possible?

   _____

3. Do you always use a seatbelt when one is available? Why or why not?

   _____

UNIT 22　Learn from the Masters

条件の if

Overview

自分の思いを芸術作品として表現してみたいと思ったことがある人も多いでしょう．この Unit は，有名な画家の作品を観察することによって描画の技術を学ぶ方法についてです．if の使い方に注意しながら，次の文章を読んでみましょう．

Text　DL 44　CD 44

　　Do you sometimes want to express yourself through art? Why not try painting? And **if** you do decide to give it a try, start by learning from some of the most famous painters of all time. It's best to visit a gallery **if** possible, but these days you can also easily find their work online.

5　　**If** you want to make your paintings realistic, try viewing the work of Gustave Courbet or Lucian Freud. Notice their attention to detail. Carefully observe their highly skillful use of shading and texture.

　　Alternatively, **if** you wish to paint like an impressionist, take a look at pieces by Monet and Renoir. Notice the brush strokes and see how their
10　paintings are so full of movement and the accurate depiction of light.

　　Or perhaps the work of Jackson Pollock, famous for his original style of drip painting, has caught your attention. **If** you choose to experiment with his style of painting, remember that he often used sticks and knives instead of brushes.

15　　Don't be afraid of being inspired by famous painters because whoever inspires you, your paintings will always be yours. In fact, there will be something special and unique about each and every one.

Glossary
to observe「観察する」　a piece「作品」　shading「影」　texture「質感」　a depiction「描写」
to be inspired「感銘・影響を受ける」

UNIT 22　*Learn from the Masters*

Understanding

英文の内容に関する答えとして正しいものを a ～ c の中から選びましょう.

1. Where is the best place to see famous paintings?
   a. in your mind　　　b. a gallery　　　c. online
2. Which word is closest in meaning to 'realistic' as it is used in the text?
   a. honest　　　b. logical　　　c. lifelike
3. What kind of painter was Monet?
   a. an impressionist　　　b. a realist　　　c. an alternative
4. Who didn't always paint with brushes?
   a. Lucian Freud　　　b. Jackson Pollock　　　c. Renoir
5. What is the main purpose of the text?
   a. to encourage the reader
   b. to criticize the reader
   c. to make the reader laugh

Collocation Finder　DL 45　CD 45

下の囲みの中の語を使って, 英文中で使われているコロケーションを完成させましょう.

> brush　highly　accurate　original　attention　by

1. an _____ depiction
2. an _____ style 
3. _____ strokes 
4. inspired _____ 
5. _____ to detail 
6. _____ skillful 

87

Grammar Watch　　　条件の if

アドバイスをする文には，条件を表す if 節が多く使われます．

If you [want / wish / decide / choose] to V …, [命令文 / let's / you can / you should / you have to / you need to] V …　「もし〜したければ，／〜すると決めたら，〜しましょう／〜できます／〜しなければならない．」

if 節と主節はどちらが先に来てもかまいません．
例▶ If you want to pass this course, you have to come to every class.
　　= Come to every class **if** you want to pass this course.
　　（このクラスの単位を取るためには毎回授業に出席すること）
　条件を表す If の節の中では，これから先のことを言う文であっても通常未来を表す will を使いません（主節の中では使います）．
例▶ If the weather is (✗ will be) good tomorrow, let's go hiking.
　　また，よく使う表現では主語＋動詞（it is）が省略される場合があります．
例▶ I'll go with you **if necessary**．（必要なら，一緒に行くよ．）
　　　You should go abroad to study **if possible**．（可能なら，留学すべきだよ．）

Grammar Try Out

日本語の意味に合うように以下の語句を並べ替え，英文を完成させましょう．

1. 芸術で自分を表現したければ，絵画を試してみてはいかが?
(you want / through art / to express yourself / try painting if)

2. 必要ならば，いつでもネットで有名な絵画を見ることができます．
(take a look / can always / paintings online / if necessary you / at famous)

3. ドリップ・ペインティングをやってみたかったら，ジャクソン・ポロックの作品を見てみましょう．
(try drip / if you want to / by Jackson Pollock / look at pieces / painting, take a)

4. 写実画に興味があるなら，細部に目をやりましょう．
(you are / pay attention / interested in / realistic paintings / to detail if)

5. 絵を描けば，その作品は常に唯一無二のものになります．
(if you / unique / work will / try painting, your / always be)

88

UNIT 22 | *Learn from the Masters*

Checkpoint

[　] 内のキーフレーズを使って日本語に合う英文を作りましょう.

1. 彼の描画スタイルは非常に独特だ.　　[**original style**]

_____

2. 彼女はもっと細部に注意を向ける必要があるだろう.　　[**pay more attention**]

_____

3. 私はこの偉大な芸術作品から多大な影響を受けている.　　[**work of art**]

_____

4. 高度な技巧を持つ画家になりたければ, 毎日練習しなければならない.

[**need to practice**]

_____

5. 有名な絵画を注意深く観察すれば, たくさんのことが学べます.　　[**look carefully**]

_____

Guided Practice

自分で言葉を補って英文を完成させましょう.

1. If you need some advice about painting, you can _____.

2. If you want to see great paintings, I recommend _____.

3. If you want to learn more about famous artists, you can _____.

4. If you paint my portrait, I will _____.

5. If people don't like your paintings, you should _____.

Open Practice

この Unit で学んだ文法（条件の if）を使って, 質問に答えましょう.

1. Where do you go if you want to see great art?

_____

2. What can you do if you want to learn to paint?

_____

3. What else can you try if you aren't interested in painting?

_____

UNIT 23

New Technology

伝達の that

Overview

技術革新により社会はますます急速に変化しています．この Unit は，これまで 100 年以上もの間変化してこなかったキーボードの新しいデザインについてです．伝達の that に注意しながら，次の文章を読んでみましょう．

Text DL 46 CD 46

　　Researchers have designed a new keyboard. They say **that** it makes "thumb-typing" easier on touchscreen devices such as tablets and large smartphones. The new keyboard design is called KALQ and it will be available for download as a free app.

5　　What is special about the new design and how is it different? First, the letters which are used most often are closer to each other. This means **that** you don't waste so much time moving your thumbs. Second, the right thumb is given all the vowels (a, e, i, o, u) and the left thumb is given more keys.

10　　Two-thumb typing is certainly very different from typing on a traditional qwerty keyboard, which was designed over 100 years ago for typewriters. And while ordinary people using a qwerty keyboard on a touchscreen device type at about 20 words per minute, on KALQ it is possible to reach 37 words per minute.

15　　The talented designers of the new keyboard claim **that** it offers a faster and more comfortable typing experience. They hope **that** many people agree and download their app.

Glossary

a device「端末（スマートフォンやタブレットなど）」　an app「（スマートフォンやタブレット端末などの）アプリ」　a vowel「母音 (a, e, i, o, u)」　qwerty「（キーボードが）通常の文字配列の（上から2列目のキーが左から q, w, e, r, t, y と並んでいることから）」　talented「才能ある，有能な」　to claim「主張する」

UNIT 23　*New Technology*

Understanding

英文の内容に関する答えとして正しいものを a～c の中から選びましょう．

1. What does the new keyboard make easier?
   a. downloading apps　　**b.** thumb-typing　　**c.** designing smartphones
2. How much does the new keyboard design cost?
   a. a lot　　**b.** not much　　**c.** nothing
3. Which thumb is used for the letters a, e, i, o and u?
   a. the left　　**b.** the right　　**c.** both
4. How much faster is it possible to type on the new keyboard?
   a. 20 words per minute
   b. 37 words per minute
   c. 17 words per minute
5. How can people get the new keyboard?
   a. download it　　**b.** buy it　　**c.** design it

Collocation Finder　DL 47　CD 47

下の囲みの中の語を使って，英文中で使われているコロケーションを完成させましょう．

download　typing　ordinary　left　keyboard　touchscreen

1. a _____ device
2. the _____ thumb 
3. _____ an app 
4. _____ people 
5. two-thumb _____ 
6. a qwerty _____ 

91

Grammar Watch　　伝達の that

誰かから聞いたことや，主張や希望を伝えるとき，say, hope, claim などの動詞と that 節を使います．that の後は普通の文のように，主語（S）＋動詞（V）を続けます．

例▶ They **say that** a typhoon will come here tomorrow.（明日台風がくるそうだ．）
　　　I **hope that** everything goes well.（すべてがうまくいきますように．）
　　　Many people **claim that** they have seen a UFO.（UFO を見たことがあると主張する人は多い．）

少し形式ばった言い方になりますが，主語を明示する必要がない場合は受動態で，It is said that…, It is hoped that…, It is claimed that… と書くこともできます．

例▶ **It is hoped that** the present study will serve as a catalyst for future investigations.（本研究が今後の調査の呼び水になることを願います．）

前の文を受けてその意味や結果などを説明するのにも that 節は使われます．

例▶ **This means that** you must pay the annual fee.（つまり年会費を払う必要があるということです．）

that 節が使えるかどうかは動詞によって決まります．辞書でその語が使える文型を確認しましょう．例えば辞書の claim の項には［SV（that）節 / SV to do］と構文が説明されています．これは claim が that 節や to 不定詞を伴って使うことができる，またその場合の that は省略可能であるということを示しています．

Grammar Try Out

日本語の意味に合うように以下の語句を並べ替え，英文を完成させましょう．

1. つまり，無料でダウンロードできるということです．
   (for free / it means / you can download it / that)

2. 多くの人が新しいキーボードを使うようになるといいですね．
   (hoped that / very popular / it is / will be / the new keyboard)

3. このことからわかるように，技術は常に変化しているのです．
   (always changing / shows that / technology is / this)

4. より快適になるだろうと言われています．
   (it will be / they claim / that / more comfortable)

5. KALQ により親指タイピングはより簡単になるそうです．
   (makes thumb-typing / that KALQ / easier / they say)

UNIT 23 | New Technology

Checkpoint

[　] 内のキーフレーズを使って日本語に合う英文を作りましょう.

1. 古いキーボードは使いにくいそうだ.　　[say that]

_____

2. 新しい製品は人気が出るだろう.　　[hope that]

_____

3. このデザインのほうがよいと主張している.　　[claim that]

_____

4. これはつまり早く打てるということだ.　　[means that]

_____

5. 将来、私たちの生活がよりよくなることを願う.　　[hoped that]

_____

Guided Practice

自分で言葉を補って文を完成させましょう.

1. I think that two-thumb typing is _____.

2. I believe that the KALQ keyboard will be _____.

3. I hope that someone designs a new _____.

4. I think that touchscreen devices are _____.

5. I believe that qwerty keyboards are _____.

Open Practice

この Unit で学んだ文法（伝達の that）を使って，質問に答えましょう.

1. What do you think of your current mobile phone?

_____

2. What do you hope that your next mobile phone will be able to do?

_____

3. What do you believe mobile devices will look like in the future?

_____

UNIT 24: Rating Professors

理由の because

Overview

学生の間で評判のいい先生は誰でしょう？ この Unit はこんな質問に答えてくれる人気のウェブサイトについてです．because の使い方に注意しながら，次の文章を読んでみましょう．

Text DL 48 CD 48

Who are the best professors at my university? One American website has become successful by asking students to rate their professors online. So, what do professors with the highest ratings have in common?

First, popular professors tend to be friendly, helpful and caring. It
5 seems that students really appreciate professors who give them individual attention, make time to answer questions and show that they genuinely care. Students frequently write comments such as, "He's great **because** he always makes himself accessible to students."

Students also think highly of professors who are entertaining and fun.
10 They often comment that they learned a lot **because** the professor was funny and tried hard to make the class enjoyable. Most students seem to understand that learning is easier when they are having a good time.

Finally, students admire professors who have the ability to explain things clearly. One student wrote, "You will love her class **because** she
15 explains everything really well!" Students certainly want to enjoy their classes, but they also know that they need to understand the contents of their courses.

Glossary

to rate 「評価する」 a rating 「ランキング，格付け」 in common 「共通している」
to appreciate 「高く評価する，ありがたく思う」 accessible 「接しやすい」
to think highly of 「〜を尊敬する，高く評価する」

UNIT 24 | Rating Professors

Understanding

英文の内容に関する答えとして正しいものをa～cの中から選びましょう．

1. What name would be appropriate for the website?
   a. Rate My Class!   b. Rate Your School!   c. Rate Your Prof!
2. Who are the main users of the website?
   a. students   b. professors   c. parents
3. Which word is closest in meaning to accessible?
   a. friendly   b. funny   c. successful
4. Why do students like professors who are entertaining?
   a. They like to laugh.
   b. They make learning easier.
   c. They give higher grades.
5. What else do students like?
   a. young professors   b. interesting content   c. clear explanations

Collocation Finder DL 49 CD 49

下の囲みの中の語を使って，英文中で使われているコロケーションを完成させましょう．

| attention | learn | clearly | genuinely | high | become |

1. to _____ successful
2. a _____ rating 
3. to _____ care 
4. to explain _____ 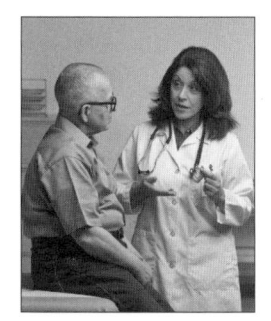
5. individual _____ 
6. to _____ a lot 

95

Grammar Watch　　　理由の because

　理由を述べるため最もよく使うのは because の節でしょう．because の節は主節の後ろに来るのが一般的です．日本人学習者が because を使った文を書くときによくある間違いは2つあります．一つは主節と理由の節が別々の文になっていて繋がっていない場合です．because の節だけでは文として成り立ちませんので必ず主節をつけましょう．

例▶　○ I was tired today **because** I stayed up till late last night.
　　　× I was tired today. **Because** I stayed up till late last night.
　　　（昨日夜更かししたから，今日は疲れていた．）

　もう一つのよくある間違いは because の節に主語と動詞が整っていない場合です．前置詞のように使う because of と違い because は接続詞ですから必ず主語と動詞が必要です．

例▶　○ I went to bed early **because** I was tired.
　　　× I went to bed early **because** tired.
　　　（疲れていたので早く寝た）

　また，日本語では理由を述べるとき，「～なので，～だから」とはっきりと理由であることを言い表さないこともあります．文の意味から理由を述べていることを読み取って because を使うという判断をする必要があることもあります．

例▶　I was late **because** I got stuck in a traffic jam.（渋滞にはまって遅れてしまった．）

Grammar Try Out

　日本語の意味に合うように以下の語句を並べ替え，英文を完成させましょう．

1. 学生達がそのサイトにアクセスするのは，先生の格付けをしたいからだ．
　(they want to / students visit / rate their professors / the website because)

_____

2. その先生は，いつも学生一人ひとりに気を配っていて，すごい．
　(she always gives / she's great / students individual / because / attention)

_____

3. その授業は楽しかったから，学生はより多くのことを学べた．
　(more because / the students / learned / the class / they enjoyed)

_____

4. あの先生の説明はわかりやすいから，学生に好かれる．
　(he's very good at / students like / explaining things clearly / him because)

_____

5. 気さくで，面倒見がよいという理由で人気の先生もいる．
　(some professors / because they / and helpful / are popular / are friendly)

_____

UNIT 24 | *Rating Professors*

⚐ Checkpoint

[　] 内のキーフレーズを使って日本語に合う英文を作りましょう．

1. おもしろい先生は学生に尊敬される． [think highly of]

　_____

2. 人気の先生には共通点が3つあることが多い． [in common]

　_____

3. 先生が親身になってくれるからこそ勉強もはかどるというものだ．
   [the professor genuinely cares]

　_____

4. 学生は一人ひとりへの配慮を高く評価する． [individual attention]

　_____

5. 楽しいだけじゃなく学ぶことも大切だと学生はわかっている． [as important as]

　_____

⚐ Guided Practice

自分で言葉を補って文を完成させましょう．

1. She was my favorite teacher in high school because _____.

2. He is my favorite professor at university because _____.

3. I decided to go to university because _____.

4. I like my English class because _____.

5. I like that website because _____.

⚐ Open Practice

このUnitで学習した文法（理由のbecause）を使って，質問に答えましょう．

1. Which website do you visit most often? Why do you visit it?

　_____

2. Which university class do you most enjoy? Why do you enjoy it?

　_____

3. What makes a good teacher? Why do you think so?

　_____

本書には音声CD（別売）があります

Express Ahead
表現のための文法で学ぶ発信型英語

2015年 1月20日　初版第1刷発行
2021年10月31日　初版第9刷発行

著　者　Graeme　Todd
　　　　Roger　Palmer
　　　　加野まきみ

発行者　福　岡　正　人
発行所　株式会社　金星堂
（〒101-0051）東京都千代田区神田神保町3-21
Tel. (03) 3263-3828（営業部）
(03) 3263-3997（編集部）
Fax (03) 3263-0716
http://www.kinsei-do.co.jp

編集担当　芦川正宏　　　　Printed in Japan
印刷所／日新印刷株式会社　製本所／松島製本
本書の無断複製・複写は著作権法上での例外を除き禁じられ
ています。本書を代行業者等の第三者に依頼してスキャンや
デジタル化することは、たとえ個人や家庭内での利用であっ
ても認められておりません。
落丁・乱丁本はお取り替えいたします。
ISBN978-4-7647-4002-0　　C1082